DAVID THE KING

FACILITATOR GUIDE

STUDY PROGRAM CHECKLIST	3
STUDY PROGRAM MATERIALS	7
PROGRAM PLANNING	9
LEADERSHIP TEAM	10
LEADERSHIP PREPARATION	11
GROUP FACILITATOR GUIDELINES	13
PROGRAM STRUCTURE OPTIONS	17
SESSION OVERVIEW	19
FILM LESSON TRACK TIMES	21
ONLINE RESOURCES	22

STUDY PROGRAM CHECKLIST

This is a summary of all the key steps Word on Fire recommends for the *David the King* Study Program. You can use it in your planning and program administration. Additional detail for each phase is provided in the remainder of this guide.

PHASE 1: PLANNING

☐ **Pray** your way through all planning and put your trust in the Holy Spirit. As St. Paul tells us in First Thessalonians, "Rejoice always. Pray without ceasing" (1 Thess. 5:16-17).

☐ At least three months before you launch the program, the Program Coordinator should **meet with the Pastor or Group Director** to secure approval and to plan the dates of the program, including the pre-program Leader's Orientation session.

☐ Identify and **reserve the place** where the program will be held. This room should include:

- A large screen and either a DVD or Blu-ray player (or a laptop and projector if you are streaming the videos from a digital subscription). If you have a big group, it is often helpful to have the screen raised for easier viewing.
- Chairs to accommodate all participants
- Break-out rooms or secluded areas for small group discussion— a separate space for each group
- Tables around which participants may gather for discussion. This allows the group to spread out materials.

☐ **Recruit other members** of the leadership team, namely the Program Administrator and Group Discussion Facilitator. You should have one Group Facilitator for every 8-10 people.

☐ **Order the Study Program Leader's Kit** about two months ahead, so the Program Coordinator can review the materials and begin to plan the Leaders' Orientation Session. You can find these at *David.wordonfire.org*.

☐ Determine if the **cost of the program materials** will be passed through to the participants. Don't forget to include shipping, handling, applicable tax, and any other expenses your program will incur in the total cost to be allocated and assigned as a registration fee. Don't hesitate to charge a registration fee, as people often value something *more* if they have to pay for it.

☐ **Publicize the *David the King* program** with free, downloadable posters and flyers found at *David.wordonfire.org/#support*

- ☐ Place an **announcement in the Sunday bulletin** that includes a registration form (also available at *David.wordonfire.org/#support*). Ask for the registration form and fee to be submitted at least three weeks ahead of the start of the program so you can order the right number of Study Guides for your group. We suggest ordering a few extra knowing that you can return them within 90 days for a full refund, if they have not been unwrapped.

- ☐ Plan at least one Sunday where the program can be **announced from the pulpit**. Set up a registration table in the vestibule staffed by the leadership team and complete with registration forms and a sample study guide. If possible, play the *David the King* trailer on a laptop, so parishioners can experience the visual impact of the study. The trailer can be found at: *DavidtheKing.com*.

- ☐ Right before the Leaders' Orientation Session, the Program Administrator should **compile a roster** of all registrants that includes contact information.

- ☐ **Assign each participant on the roster to a Group Facilitator** (to be announced at Leaders' Orientation). Try to balance age, gender, and adult formation experience, so each group has a diverse mix. Also, if you know many of the registrants, try to balance the "talkers" with the "listeners."

- ☐ Hold the **Facilitators' Orientation Session** one to two weeks ahead of the start of the program. See details in the Leadership Preparation section on page 11.

PHASE 2: HOSTING THE PROGRAM

☐ **Pray** your way through all planning and put your trust in the Holy Spirit. As St. Paul tells us in First Thessalonians, "Rejoice always. Pray without ceasing" (1 Thess. 5:16-17).

☐ **First session: Welcome and Orientation**. Create an atmosphere where people can comfortably orient themselves to the program and get to know their small groups.

☐ **Begin Leadership Prep Meetings** before the second session. Meet to pray, review *Questions for Understanding,* and discuss any administrative issues.

☐ Make sure there is **a way for participants to ask questions** that might remain after the group discussion. If you have a priest or deacon involved, questions may be directed to him. If you do not have access to a priest or deacon, you can send unanswered questions to: *StudyPrograms@wordonfire.org.*

☐ **Encourage the Group Facilitators to contact each of their group members** regularly outside of the program session. Group Facilitators can call, email, or connect with participants in person. This contact is important to build fellowship among the small groups, to uncover any concerns, and to promote trust and openness. Remember, evangelization starts with a loving *relationship* of mutual trust.

PHASE 3: EVALUATION AND NEXT STEPS

- ☐ **PRAY** your way through evaluation and put your trust in the Holy Spirit.

- ☐ Revise and/or hand out the survey (found at *David.wordonfire.org/#support*) a few sessions before the program ends. Encourage all participants and leaders to complete the survey, so you can continually improve your Adult Formation programs.

- ☐ Share any comments or suggestions with Word on Fire by emailing: *StudyPrograms@wordonfire.org*.

- ☐ Discuss options for your next Adult Formation Program. Word on Fire offers other study programs based on Bishop Barron's films. For more information on these programs, please visit *www.wordonfire.org/study-programs/*

STUDY PROGRAM MATERIALS

Everyone will need to have a Catholic translation of the Bible and access to the *Catechism of the Catholic Church* to complete the questions in each lesson. Catholic translations include:

- **Revised Standard Version:** A more literal translation used for serious Scripture study
- **New American Bible:** Used in the liturgy and is easier to read
- **New Jerusalem Bible:** More contemporary language, but still true to the original meaning

To look up references in the *Catechism of the Catholic Church*, you can purchase a copy of the *Catechism* or go to this website and enter the paragraph number to display the text: *www.scborromeo.org/ccc.htm*

Each person must have his or her own Study Guide, so everyone can write answers to the questions and take notes individually. The copying of lessons, without permission, is strictly forbidden by copyright laws.

It is suggested that each Group Facilitator have a Leader's Guide, complete with the Facilitator Guide and Answer Key.

Every lesson follows the same format:

> <u>Outline</u>: Follows the video presentation, so it can be useful for taking notes.
>
> <u>Commentary</u>: Expands on and captures much of the content presented in the video. Contains all the information that is useful in answering the *Questions for Understanding*.
>
> <u>Questions for Understanding</u>: Answers can be found in the video presentation, the study guide commentary, the Bible, and the *Catechism of the Catholic Church*. Participants should be encouraged to write down their answers as research shows that the simple act of writing something down significantly increases retention. Each discussion session should cover all of the *Questions for Understanding*, so please budget your time accordingly.
>
> <u>Questions for Application</u>: Each discussion should include **at least two** *Questions for Application*. Group facilitators can assign specific questions the week before, so participants can prepare those that will be discussed. If some of the questions seem too personal, please still encourage your participants to think about them and to pray and reflect upon them privately. The study program provides many opportunities for enrichment of each person's spiritual life, whether in a group or individually.
>
> <u>Glossary</u>: Defines theological and other terms used.

DAVID THE KING

Additional materials included in the Study Program Leader's Kit can be used to enrich and supplement the videos and study guides. These additional materials include:

2 Samuel **by Bishop Robert Barron**

- One copy of this book is included in the Leader's Kit to support the program's lay leadership. This book provides chapter-by-chapter commentary on 2 Samuel, so it can be used to help answer participant questions or to add detail to the video and/or study guide commentary. Additional copies of this book can be purchased at *wordonfire.org/resources/store.*

Called to Kingship **booklet**

- Twenty *Called to Kingship* booklets are included in the Leader's Kit, and each participant should receive one. Additional booklets can be purchased at *wordonfire.org/resources/store*. The booklet is designed to encourage participants to reflect on each baptized Christian's call to be a king in Christ. Program leaders can use these booklets in several ways:

  1. If you are using **Option 1- Program Structure**, distribute *Called to Kingship* booklets at Orientation and allow each person to read and answer the questions individually for 30 minutes. Then meet in the small groups to discuss the questions. This sets the tone for the study and makes it more personal when everyone realizes that each Christian is baptized into kingship with Christ. It also is good practice for reading the commentary and preparing the questions for each lesson to come.

  2. If you are following **Option 2**, you can use the last part of the 7th session to read and discuss the booklet in the small groups.

  3. Host a celebration and sharing session with a potluck lunch or dinner following the last lesson. Ask people to share how the study has encouraged them to take up their kingly role in their own community. Participants should read the booklet before the celebration.

  4. Encourage participants to read and reflect on this content during the study anytime at their convenience.

Answer Key

- Provided for the Group Facilitator as part of the Leader's Guide, this resource gives an in-depth answer to each *Question for Understanding*. It is not intended to be a "black-and-white, right-or-wrong" checklist against which all participants' responses are judged. Therefore, please be cautious when sharing this information, as some participants may become discouraged if they perceive that they should produce the same answer.

PROGRAM PLANNING

1. Set up the dates and times for the program according to procedures in your parish or group. Make sure to discuss the program plans with your pastor or group leader.

   It is helpful to publish a complete calendar for the program that includes each session's date and what will be covered in that session.

2. Assemble your Leadership Team (see next page).

3. Announce the program to the parish or group.
   Free materials are available at *David.wordonfire.org/#support*. These include:

   - flyer
   - poster
   - bulletin/pulpit announcement
   - registration form
   - evaluation form
   - certificate of completion

4. Strive to have one Sunday set aside where the program can be announced from the pulpit at all Masses, and parishioners can register as they leave Mass.

   Have one of your group facilitators set up a table in the vestibule at each Mass, and provide registration forms and a sample Study Guide for review. If possible, run the *David the King* trailer on a laptop, so parishioners can experience the visual impact of the study. The trailer can be found at *David.wordonfire.org*.

5. Run an announcement in the Bulletin, which should include a registration form. Provide a deadline for registration that is at least three weeks before your first session, so you can order Study Guides for all participants. Study Guides can be returned within 90 days for a full refund as long as they are unused and still shrink-wrapped. You might want to order a few more than you think you will need, as most groups have walk-in participants at the first session.

6. Supply and collect registration forms, so you know how many will participate and can order enough Study Guides. You should also collect a registration fee to cover the materials. It's human nature to value what you pay for more than something that is free, so don't hesitate to charge for the program. A registration form template can be downloaded at *David.wordonfire.org/#support*.

DAVID THE KING

LEADERSHIP TEAM

The three key roles on the Leadership Team are:

- Program Coordinator
- Program Administrator
- Small Group Facilitator

PROGRAM COORDINATOR:

- Manages the overall program and is the key contact for the pastor and parish
- Plans and executes the promotion of the study program
- Begins each session with prayer and announcements when all are assembled as a group
- Recruits Group Facilitators with the approval of the pastor or supervisor of the community
- Addresses issues and concerns of participants if they arise

PROGRAM ADMINISTRATOR:

- Manages the registration process, including finances for the group
- Orders and distributes materials
- Develops a roster that lists all participants and their contact information
- Makes nametags for each participant and Group Facilitator

SMALL GROUP FACILITATOR:

- Facilitates discussion of study guide questions with group of 8-10 participants
- Takes attendance each session and contacts members who miss frequently to discern if issues are present
- Contacts each member each week outside of class via phone, email, or in person
- Program Coordinator and Administrator can also serve as Group Facilitators

LEADERSHIP PREPARATION

A few weeks before the start of your *David the King* program, plan to host a **Leaders' Orientation Session**. This can be accomplished in about two hours and should include the following:

Prayer and Spiritual Enrichment: Invite a priest or experienced speaker to lead a 45-60 minute spiritual enrichment session. This could be on any facet of the Church and should include some assigned reading from Scripture or specific writings. The purpose of this time is to grow spiritually and prepare for the mission of adult formation and evangelization.

Program Overview: Explain the structure of the *David the King* program, including the leadership meetings before each session and the unique activities that will be part of the First Session (Participant Orientation). Give each facilitator his/her own Study Program Leader's Guide, which contains this Facilitator's Guide, all the lessons, and the Answer Key. Ask the leadership team to briefly review the materials before the program starts.

Group Facilitator's Role: Review and discuss as a group the section of this guide that explains the role of a Group Facilitator when you are together at this meeting. Reinforce that the leader is a *facilitator*, not a teacher or expert.

Group Assignment: Give each leader a list of his or her members and contact information. *Word on Fire* suggests that you pre-assign groups, so friends and spouses do not sit together. It is important that each member comes to their discussion group as an individual and forms new bonds within this group. Pre-existing relationships have certain communication patterns and "inside connections" that could create a clique-like atmosphere, which will work against group cohesion.

Once the groups are assigned, ask each facilitator to contact his or her members for a friendly introduction and to provide a reminder about the first session's date and time.

Administrative Tasks: You can enlist your leadership team to help with tasks that are necessary to prepare for the first session (e.g., making name tags, unpacking study guides, preparing "get to know you" exercises for the first session, etc.)

Leadership Prep Meeting Planning: Begin regular preparation meetings with the leadership team before the second session. This meeting should be held before each of the six general sessions to pray together and also to help the Group Facilitators prepare to lead their groups by going through the *Questions for Understanding* together.

During each Leadership Prep Meeting (60-75 minutes) plan to:

1. **Pray as a team** for the program as a whole and for any individual intentions. These meetings should begin and end with prayer. Often, Facilitators will bring the needs of individuals in their small groups to prayer at these meetings.

2. **Review** the *Questions for Understanding*. When the Facilitators spend some time discussing their own responses and all the resources they uncovered to answer the questions, they will be much better prepared to facilitate their own small groups.

3. **Discuss** any administrative or other issues.

GROUP FACILITATOR GUIDELINES

Role:

You are Christ's representative to your small group. As a Leader, people will look to you to model Christ's attitudes and behavior and to also be loyal and true to the teachings of his Church. During the study, enrich your own spiritual life by spending more time in prayer, attending Mass more frequently, and receiving the Sacraments regularly.

You are a facilitator, not a teacher or expert. You are called to facilitate discussion of the study guide questions in the small groups, not to teach the material or give your own answers to the questions. Use the resources provided in the Leader's Kit, especially the Study Guide Commentary and the Answer Key, to guide your group to more fully understand the content of each lesson. The philosophy of this approach is that we are all adults learning together with Bishop Barron as our "teacher," under the guidance of the Holy Spirit. Group Leaders facilitate this learning without becoming experts or teachers themselves. If there are outstanding questions at the end of the group discussion, you should first seek out a priest or deacon for guidance. In addition, Word on Fire can help with questions when emailed to **StudyPrograms@WordOnFire.org**. However, it may take up to two weeks to receive a response as our qualified staff is small. Another great resource for questions is the *Catholic Answers* forum (forums.catholic.com).

You are the shepherd of the group. Help each member feel comfortable. Keep discussion focused on the questions for that lesson. Lead with love and a positive attitude of acceptance of each person's worth in Christ.

Your goal is to create and maintain positive group dynamics in the discussion. Some groups may have one or more challenging people that you will have to manage within the group discussion or talk to privately. Please review *Managing Personalities* in the Support Materials section at *David.wordonfire.org/#support*.

Responsibilities:

1. Outside of class time, **pray for your group** collectively and as individuals. Also, before beginning the discussion of the lesson, say a short prayer with the group.

2. **Be watchful for "contrary spirits."** Increase your own prayer time and reception of the Sacraments, especially the Eucharist, to access God's grace to fortify your leadership.

DAVID THE KING — 13

3. **Create a relaxed, warm atmosphere of acceptance and eagerness to learn from one another.**

   - Get to know your members. Contact them outside of class two or three times during the program to build relationships and answer any questions they may have.
   - Maintain eye contact in the group.
   - Reassure that "we are all learning together."
   - Encourage the use of name tags.

4. **Establish that you are the facilitator and leader of the discussion.**

   - If your group is assembled around a table, sit at the head of the table. If seated at a round table or in a circle of chairs, sit in the chair facing the door and leave the spot opposite you open (i.e., in a horseshoe-type pattern)
   - If possible, face the door so you can welcome late-comers
   - To ensure positive group dynamics, manage personalities within the group or by talking to the person privately. Some helpful tips can be found in the *Managing Personalities* summary in the Support Materials section at *David.wordonfire.org/#support*.

5. **Act as a facilitator, not as a teacher or expert.**

   - <u>Draw answers from your group; refrain from teaching</u>. Refrain from sharing your own opinions and answers to the *Questions for Understanding*. Remain neutral as much as possible, so members feel they can express differing thoughts and not look for the leader's answer as affirmation. Be patient when there is silence. Don't jump in with answers, but you can rephrase the question or ask probing questions to foster dialogue.

   - <u>Use discernment in handling misconceptions</u>. Try to tactfully bring out the truth according to the Church's teaching. It is useful to ask for other opinions among the group if an answer seems confusing or does not reflect the truth of God's word.

   - <u>Keep track of time</u>. Lessons should be completed during your allotted time. Avoid getting off the subject — stick with the lesson. In each discussion session, the Facilitator is responsible for finishing **all** of the *Questions for Understanding*, and as many *Questions for Application* as possible.

   - <u>Use the Answer Key carefully.</u> It will add insight to the group discussion. Do not present the Answer Key as the standard to which the group is supposed to attain in their written pre-work. The Answer Key is much more detailed than any one participant's answers and brings in information from sources not available to the group. Please do NOT photocopy and hand out the Answer Key as this can set up unrealistic expectations for each participant's contributions.

   - All the questions can be answered from the film lessons, the Commentary in the Study Guide, and from the references provided to the Bible passages and the *Catechism*. The small group discussion will be much more fruitful if participants complete the questions in writing before the discussion.

6. **Promote participation by all group members.**

   During the first session, develop some ground rules for participation. It's helpful to prepare your group with an understanding of the overall program. Please set expectations at a high level so the participants can truly commit to grow into better disciples and evangelists.

   Some suggestions to share with the participants for setting expectations and ground rules for discussion:

   - **Pray**: Ask for guidance from the Holy Spirit and keep an open mind.

   - **Commit to the study**: Plan to come each time and stay for the whole session. Obviously emergencies come up, but the goal is to begin the study with an attitude of commitment to attend all sessions. Encourage completion of lessons even if someone misses the session. It's helpful to have an extra set of the film series to lend to those who need to make up a session.

   - **Everyone participates:** The Facilitator may say something like, "If you tend to talk a lot, please listen more. If you prefer to listen, please pick at least one of your answers to share with the group. Questions are welcome—don't feel you have to have the answer to talk."

   - **Be prepared:** Stress the importance of reading the Commentary and writing down answers to the questions; however, tell them to come even if they didn't have time to prepare. They will still benefit from hearing others discuss the lesson and from watching the video. Encourage members to complete their lessons when they are absent so they can keep up with the study. You may want a second set of videos to lend when someone misses a session. Or, you can suggest that they purchase a digital subscription to *David the King* at wordonfire.org/resources/store, if they would like access to all the videos.

   - **Guarantee confidentiality:** All things discussed in the group are to be kept confidential. This is very important, especially for the *Questions for Application* in each lesson.

PROGRAM STRUCTURE OPTIONS

NUMBER OF SESSIONS: **Seven**

DURATION OF EACH SESSION: **90 minutes**

PROGRAM FLOW:
There are two options for presenting this program in seven sessions as summarized in the chart below. Option #1 requires individual preparation before viewing the film lesson, while Option #2 requires individual preparation after viewing the film lesson.

	STRUCTURE OPTION #1	STRUCTURE OPTION #2
1ST SESSION (PARTICIPANT ORIENTATION)	- Orientation Activities (see below) - Assign *Law of the Gift* reading/questions—Lesson 1	- Orientation Activities (see below) - Show *Law of the Gift* - Assign *Law of the Gift* reading/questions—Lesson 1
2ND SESSION	- Show *Law of the Gift* video - Discuss *Law of the Gift* questions - Assign *Your Servant is Listening* reading/questions	- Discuss *Law of the Gift* questions - Show *Your Servant is Listening* video - Assign *Your Servant is Listening* reading/questions
3RD SESSION	- Show *Your Servant is Listening* video - Discuss *Your Servant is Listening* questions - Assign *Warrior of God* reading/questions	- Discuss *Your Servant is Listening* questions - Show *Warrior of God* video - Assign *Warrior of God* reading/questions
4TH SESSION	- Show *Warrior of God* video - Discuss *Warrior of God* questions - Assign *Gathered in Jerusalem* reading/questions	- Discuss *Warrior of God* questions - Show *Gathered in Jerusalem* video - Assign *Gathered in Jerusalem* reading/questions
5TH SESSION	- Show *Gathered in Jerusalem* video - Discuss *Gathered in Jerusalem* questions - Assign *The House of David* reading/questions	- Discuss *Gathered in Jerusalem* questions - Show *The House of David* video - Assign *The House of David* reading/questions
6TH SESSION	- Show *The House of David* video - Discuss *The House of David* questions - Assign *Absalom, My Son!* reading/questions	- Discuss *The House of David* questions - Show *Absalom, My Son!* video - Assign *Absalom, My Son!* reading/questions
7TH SESSION	- Show *Absalom, My Son!* video - Discuss *Absalom, My Son!* questions	- Discuss *Absalom, My Son!* questions

DAVID THE KING

FIRST SESSION ACTIVITIES

Orientation:

- Confirm pre-registered participants
- Register walk-ins
- Distribute Study Guides and nametags to all (Note: order 15-20% more than pre-registrations for unexpected "walk-ins" during the first few sessions).
- Opening Prayer
- Present overview of Program Structure, explaining the session flow for either Option #1 or Option #2 above.
- Present Program Expectations to entire group (examples on page 15).
- Meet in the assigned small discussion groups for introductions and discussion of Ground Rules for Group Discussion (examples on page 15).
- For introductions, you could use an ice-breaker game, such as:

    "Tell us one thing that is true about you and one that is false." (The rest of group guesses which is which.)
    "What is your favorite Old Testament story and why?"
    "Why did you decide to register for this program? What are your expectations?"

- In your small groups, discuss the *Called to Kingship* booklet **or** skim through Lesson 1- *The Law of the Gift* in the Study Guide. Make sure the participants understand what they need to do before the next session.

SESSION OVERVIEW

1. **Gathering and Opening** (5 minutes)

   Many groups offer refreshments and encourage their participants to come a few minutes early for some time of fellowship. The Program Coordinator should begin the session promptly. It is very important to start and finish on time.

   If you have a priest or deacon participating, he can lead the Opening Prayer and offer a few words related to the session topic. Try to avoid another lecture here—the film serves as the "lecture" and teaching part of the program. You can also sing a hymn together to set a reverent tone.

   The Prayer to the Holy Spirit (below) is an appropriate prayer to use to begin each session.

   > *Come Holy Spirit. Fill the hearts of your faithful*
   > *And kindle in them the fire of your love.*
   > *Send forth your Spirit and they shall be created*
   > *And you shall renew the face of the earth.*
   >
   > *Oh God, who by the light of the Holy Spirit,*
   > *Did instruct the hearts of the faithful,*
   > *Grant that by the same Holy Spirit*
   > *We may be truly wise and ever enjoy his consolations*
   > *Through Christ, our Lord. Amen.*

   Also, the Prayer to St. Michael the Archangel has been used by some groups to seek spiritual protection:

   > *St. Michael the Archangel, defend us in battle.*
   > *Be our protection against the wickedness and snares of the Devil.*
   > *May God rebuke him, we humbly pray,*
   > *And do thou, O Prince of the heavenly hosts, by the power of God,*
   > *Cast into hell Satan, and all the evil spirits*
   > *Who roam through the world*
   > *Seeking the destruction of souls. Amen.*

   You can copy these prayers so everyone can join in.

   During the first session (Orientation), the Program Coordinator should present the Program Expectations. Each small Group Facilitator should discuss their own ground rules for their group. Examples of both can be found on page 15.

DAVID THE KING

2. **Film Viewing** (20-25 minutes)

    - **Structure Option #1:** Film viewed in same session as discussion. Viewing starts in Session #2.
    - **Structure Option #2:** Film viewed the session before the discussion. Viewing starts in Session #1.

       The entire group of participants comes together to watch the film. While watching, participants can follow along and take notes using the chapter outline at the beginning of each lesson.

3. **Discussion Groups** (60 minutes)

    - **Structure Option #1:** Discussion happens during the same session as the companion film lesson is viewed (question prep before film viewing)
    - **Structure Option #2:** Discussion happens the session after the companion film lesson is viewed (question prep after film viewing)

       Break into small groups for discussion of the *Questions for Understanding* and at least one or two *Questions for Application*. If you find that you do not have time to complete all the *Questions for Application*, it is helpful to let participants know ahead of time which Application questions you will discuss.

       While the Group Facilitator should not provide any answers to the *Questions for Understanding*, he or she should share during the *Questions for Application* in order to build trust and fellowship within the small group.

4. **Closing Prayer** (<5 minutes)

    - Please use a closing prayer of your own choosing. Depending on which Program Structure Option you follow, the closing prayer will be said either in the small groups (Option #1) or with the whole group after viewing the video (Option #2).

FILM LESSON CHAPTER TIMES

DISC 1:

Lesson 1: *The Law of the Gift* (22:53)

Lesson 2: *Your Servant is Listening* (21:20)

Lesson 3: *Warrior of God* (24:06)

DISC 2:

Lesson 4: *Gathered in Jerusalem* (20:35)

Lesson 5: *The House of David* (20:50)

Lesson 6: *Absalom, My Son!* (25:27)

ONLINE RESOURCES

The following resources can be found online at *David.wordonfire.org/#support*:

Advertising

- Poster
- Flyer
- Bulletin Announcement
- Announcement from the Pulpit

Study Program Support

- Registration Form
- Certificate of Completion
- Evaluation Survey
- *Managing Personalities for Effective Group Discussion*

DAVID THE KING

STUDY GUIDE

STUDY GUIDE DIVIDER IMAGE
King David. Valentin de Boulogne, 1626-1627.
Montreal, Musée des Beaux-Arts de Montréal.

DAVID THE KING

STUDY GUIDE

A Catholic Study Program presented by
MOST REV. ROBERT E. BARRON

Study Guide written by
DR. JACOB WOOD

www.WORDONFIRE.org

© 2017 Word on Fire Catholic Ministries

DAVID THE KING

TABLE OF CONTENTS

Lesson One:	The Law of the Gift	1
Lesson Two:	Your Servant is Listening	17
Lesson Three:	Warrior of God	35
Lesson Four:	Gathered in Jerusalem	53
Lesson Five:	House of David	69
Lesson Six:	Absalom, My Son!	87

BIOGRAPHICAL INFORMATION 105

Bishop Robert Barron
Dr. Jacob Wood

GLOSSARY 107

DAVID THE KING

LESSON ONE
THE LAW OF THE GIFT

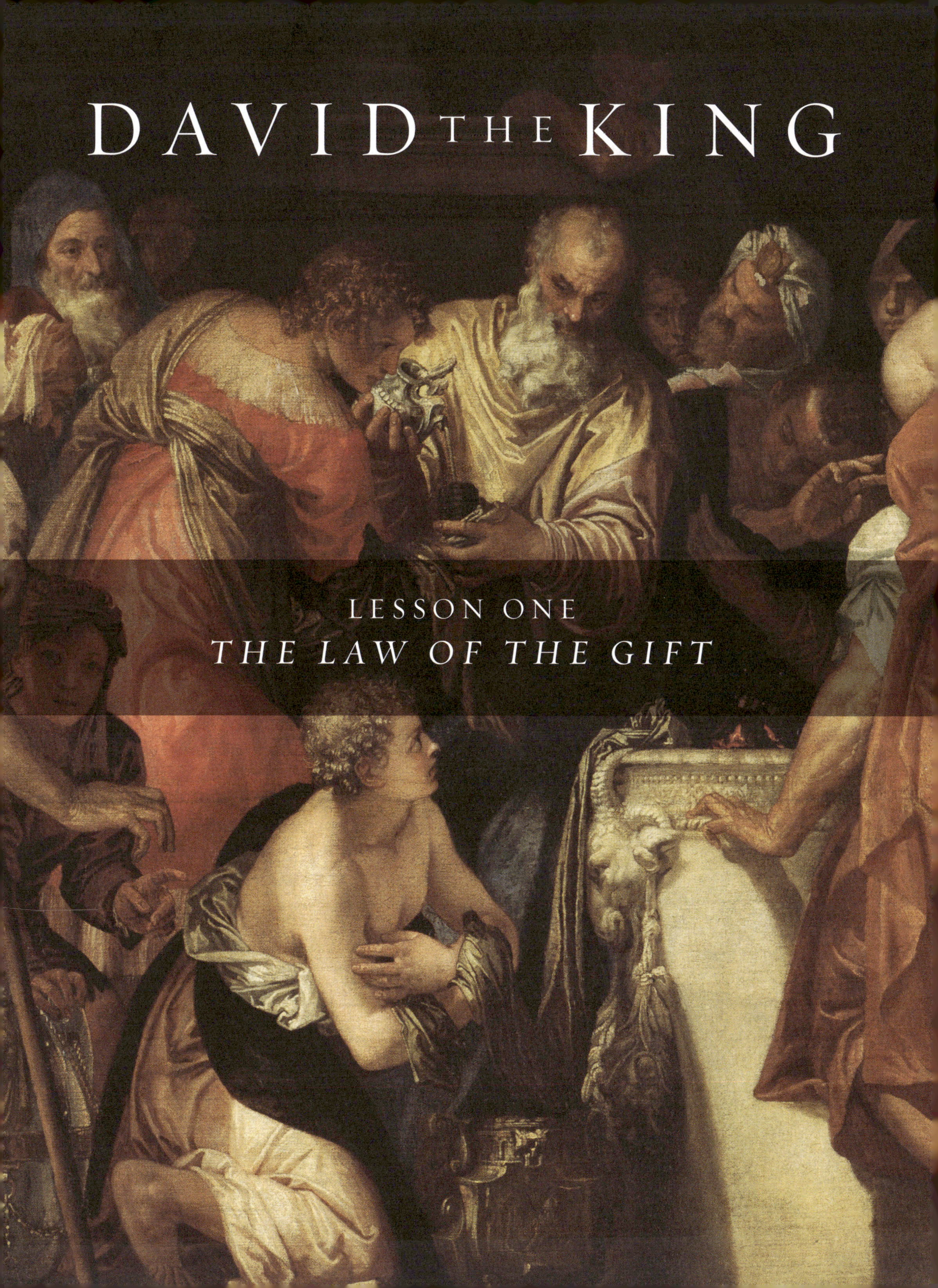

LESSON ONE IMAGE
The Anointing of David. Paolo Veronese, 1555.
Vienna, Austria. Kunsthistorisches Museum.

THE LAW OF THE GIFT
LESSON ONE OUTLINE

I. 1 & 2 SAMUEL
   A. Psychological perceptiveness and literary quality
   B. Originally one story, but translated on two scrolls
   C. Unknown authorship. Martin Noth's theory—same author for Book of Deuteronomy through 2 Kings ("Deuteronomistic Historian")

II. THEME OF KINGSHIP
   A. Adam
   B. David
   C. Jesus Christ

III. HANNAH'S STORY
   A. Hannah is pivotal to salvation history
   B. Hannah is barren and held in disregard
   C. Hannah prays for a child and interacts with Eli
   D. Hannah bears a son, Samuel, and consecrates him to the Temple
   E. God often enters through the weakest parts of life

IV. THE "LAW OF THE GIFT"
   A. "Your being increases in the measure you give it away."
   B. Hannah's song
   C. Biblical family values

Your life increases the more you give away

LESSON ONE

THE LAW OF THE GIFT

In this first talk, Bishop Barron does two things for us. First, he introduces the text of 1 and 2 Samuel and gives us a general orientation to it. Second, he discusses the theological significance of the figure of Hannah.

INTRODUCTION

As Bishop Barron was unpacking some background information about 1 and 2 Samuel, drawing illusions to the classical epic poems of Greek literature and introducing characters, perhaps you may have found yourself asking: "If Scripture is, as the Church teaches, a place in which the Father speaks to his children (*Dei Verbum* 21), why not just dive straight into the text and start applying it to our lives right away?"

There are actually two good reasons why Bishop Barron's introduction is essential if we want to come to a deep understanding of how God speaks to us in the text. Both are related to what Bishop Barron calls God's "non-competitive activity."

When Bishop Barron says that God's action is "non-competitive" with ours, he means that God prefers to work *with* us, not *against* us (CCC 306). For example, when God wanted to bring perfection to the earth he had made, he didn't just snap his fingers and make it perfect; he made Adam and Eve to till and keep it. From that point forward it wasn't as though God, Adam, and Eve had to fight over who got to do the gardening! God worked with and through Adam and Eve; their work was his work, and the perfection they brought to the garden was his perfection. There was no competition between God and humanity. Adam and Eve had what the Greek Orthodox theologian John Zizioulas calls a "priestly vocation." God gave creation to Adam and Eve so that they could perfect it by their work and make an offering of it back to him. As Bishop Barron points out, this is what it meant for Adam and Eve to have "dominion" over the earth (CCC 307).

DAVID THE KING

It is similar with the Sacred Scriptures. God created the world to be in a relationship with him, and just as God asked the people he had made to work with him in perfecting it, so likewise he asked the people he made to work with him in speaking to it. First he did this on a person-to-person basis. God spoke directly to Adam, to Eve, to Noah, to Abraham, to Isaac, to Jacob, to Moses, and to countless other people so that they could announce their encounter with him to their families, their friends, their tribes, their nations, and ultimately to the world. In the fullness of time, he sent his Son, Jesus, who spoke to the apostles so that they too might announce to the world their encounter with the Word made flesh. It is that encounter which constitutes God's Revelation first and foremost, as Bl. John Henry Newman observed in the nineteenth century in the *Grammar of Assent*, and as the Church subsequently taught at the Second Vatican Council (DV 4).

God's many encounters with his people led to writings that would bear witness to the definitive structure that the relationship had taken and would take. Here, too, he wanted to work with us and through us, so he selected specific people and gave them the charism of *inspiration*, the gift of making his words their words. That's precisely how the Bible came about. But how did God make human words his words? The answer is as simple as it is mysterious: he gave certain people a special grace, so that what they said would be infallibly what he was saying.

This does not mean that God put the human authors of Sacred Scripture in a kind of unconscious state and forcibly took over their hands. God had no fear that if they put too much of their own thought into it the text it would somehow get corrupted and would not be his anymore. Since God made human reason, he had nothing to fear from working through people who used their reason. Thus, the Church teaches that when God gave the human authors of Sacred Scripture the grace of inspiration, they acted as "true authors" (DV 11) in full possession of their reason and authorial creativity (CCC 106).

The human authors of Sacred Scripture are therefore in one sense no different than the authors of any other great work of literature; they lived in a specific place at a specific time and flourished in a specific culture. Just as you would want to know about thirteenth-century Italy when reading Dante or sixteenth-century England when reading Shakespeare, it helps

©2017 Word on Fire Catholic Ministries

to know about the historical and cultural milieu of the human authors of Scripture if you want to understand the books that they wrote under the inspiration of God (CCC 110). It's a point that St. Augustine recognized even in the fourth century: since the Sacred Scriptures are written by human beings and bear witness to human life, we need to make use of all of the human sciences to understand them fully: history, art, philology, archaeology—the list goes on! (*De doctrina Christiana* 2).

The first reason we need an introduction, then, has to do with the human author. Who was the human author of the books of Samuel? When and where did he or she compose the books?

Even with all the tools that the human disciplines afford us, it is not easy to nail down the answers to all the questions we might have about the human authors of the Old Testament. As Bishop Barron informs us, authorship in the Ancient Near East was not as simple as authorship is today. For a start, many of the books of Scripture have not come down to us with a name attached to them, and even those that have, like Joshua, Ruth, and the two books of Samuel, are more than likely named for the people they speak *about* than the people who wrote them. Even within individual books of the Old Testament, many scholars hypothesize that there may have been multiple inspired hands at work, contributing by God's grace and providence to the finished work as the Church has received it. For example, although ancient Jewish and Christian tradition ascribes the authorship of the Pentateuch (the first five books of the Old Testament) to Moses, since the nineteenth century most scholars accept some variation of Julius Wellhausen's hypothesis that at least four human authors had a hand in writing the Pentateuch, and that none of them were Moses.

One of Wellhausen's hypothetical sources was called the "Deuteronomist." The Deuteronomist was thought to be a person or persons writing in the sixth century BC. By that time, God's people, Israel, had undergone a number of difficult trials. After reaching a Golden Age of fidelity to the Lord and abundant blessings of culture, wealth, prestige, and power during the reign of Kings David and Solomon in the late eleventh and early tenth centuries BC, Israel's fidelity to the Lord waned. Under Solomon's successor, Rehoboam, the kingdom split. The ten northern tribes broke off and became the Kingdom of Israel; the two southern tribes remained as the Kingdom of Judah. Israel was conquered by the Assyrian Empire in about 721 BC and carried off into captivity. In 586 BC, the Babylonian Empire did the same to Judah. It was during that time, Wellhausen thought, that the Deuteronomist made his contribution to the Pentateuch.

The Deuteronomist, Wellhausen argued, interpreted the history of God's people in terms of the covenant that God established with Moses on Mount Sinai. That covenant, including the

Mosaic Law, promised blessings for fidelity to the Lord and threatened curses for infidelity.

> See, I have today set before you life and good, death and evil. If you obey the commandments of the LORD, your God, which I am giving you today, loving the LORD, your God, and walking in his ways, and keeping his commandments, statutes and ordinances, you will live and grow numerous, and the LORD, your God, will bless you in the land you are entering to possess. If, however, your heart turns away and you do not obey, but are led astray and bow down to other gods and serve them, I tell you today that you will certainly perish; you will not have a long life on the land which you are crossing the Jordan to enter and possess. I call heaven and earth today to witness against you: I have set before you life and death, the blessing and the curse. Choose life, then, that you and your descendants may live, by loving the LORD, your God, obeying his voice, and holding fast to him. For that will mean life for you, a long life for you to live on the land which the LORD swore to your ancestors, to Abraham, Isaac, and Jacob, to give to them. (Deut 30:15-20)

Unfortunately, the people were not ultimately faithful to their covenant relationship with the Lord. During the period of the Babylonian captivity, they understood themselves to have received the curse that Deuteronomy records in response to a period of infidelity that was so great, it even involved the loss of the Book of Deuteronomy itself!

After Wellhausen, scholars debated what to make of the historical material that comes immediately after Deuteronomy: Joshua, Judges, Ruth, 1-2 Samuel, and 1-2 Kings. Where did it come from? When was it written? Many supposed that it was a collection of stories from disparate times and places. But in 1943, the Old Testament scholar Martin Noth argued convincingly that the books had such a similar style and set of themes that they seemed to come from the same human source, a source similar to or identical with the Deuteronomist from the Pentateuch. Noth called this source the "Deuteronomistic Historian."

©2017 Word on Fire Catholic Ministries

The Deuteronomistic Historian, he argued, did not just give the basis in the Law for Israel's exile and captivity. He also provided the people with an entire account of their history, read in terms of their covenant relationship to the Lord, which explained and culminated in their Babylonian Captivity. In that context, fidelity to the Deuteronomic Covenant became the rule by which Israel's kings, its society, and all of its history were measured; it also became the key to how the people understood themselves at any given time.

Noth's hypothesis convinced scholars to read 1-2 Samuel as part of an integral whole, a story which tells of the development of the Israelite people from their entry into the Promised Land of Canaan (Joshua), their establishment as a tribal people under a series of judges (Judges), their transformation into a kingdom and ascent to power (1-2 Samuel), and their peak and decline through the Assyrian and Babylonian captivities (1-2 Kings).

Moreover, as Bishop Barron observes, this approach to the text is supported by its manuscript history. In Hebrew, there was originally only one book of Samuel—the division into two books was adopted when the text was translated into Greek because it would not fit on a single scroll. From there, since the early Latin translations of the Bible were based upon the Greek, and since St. Jerome followed the early Latin conventions when he standardized the Latin Vulgate, the division of the Book of Samuel into 1 and 2 Samuel became customary in both the Eastern (Greek) and Western (Latin) Church.

We should read 1-2 Samuel, then, as part of a single story. That story is the history of Israel from the Deuteronomic Covenant under Moses until the Babylonian Captivity, when the people of Judah received the curse of the Deuternomic Covenant. 1-2 Samuel tells the story of how that people went from a tribal federation to a kingdom, and takes us almost to Israel's peak of its fidelity to the covenant and its flourishing as a kingdom.

A second reason why an introduction is essential to understanding 1-2 Samuel is that the meaning of the text does not stop with what was in the mind of the human author when he or she composed it, nor does it stop with the end of that author's story at the Babylonian Captivity. The Church teaches that, on account of the charism of inspiration, God is just as much the author of the text as is the person who first put the pen on the paper (or the stylus on the papyrus, as the case may have been) (DV 11; CCC 105). The meaning of the text extends far beyond what the human author thought to all the things that the Holy Spirit wants to say (CCC 111). We also need an introduction so that we can know how to arrive at the Holy Spirit's intention in the text.

It is tempting to think that the human meaning of the text and the divine meaning of the text can be separated from one another, that we can bypass the difficulty of understanding the human meaning of the text and skip straight to the divine meaning. That would surely be convenient if it were possible, but it is something that the Church warns us not to do (DV 12; CCC 116). If the divine meaning of Scripture were completely separated from the human meaning, then the human authors of Scripture would not be God's willing cooperators. If God simply used them to say things that had nothing to do with what they intended, then however much God may have appeared to have gained their willing consent and participation, he would in reality have been, in a sense, tricking them into doing and saying what they did not attend to do and say.

God gave a special grace to the human authors of Sacred Scripture so that they would do two things:

1) They would intend his principal meaning, which is called the literal sense of the Scripture.

2) They would be open to his other intended meanings (the allegorical, tropological, and anagogical senses of Scripture).

INTERPRETING SACRED SCRIPTURE

The "principal meaning" of Scripture is what the tradition calls the "literal sense." The literal sense is not a "plain sense" and it is not necessarily a "historical sense." It is not a plain sense because every passage of Scripture has a literal sense, but not every passage of Scripture is plain. Some passages of Scripture are very, very difficult to understand; others are ambiguous at first glance (St. Augustine, *De doctrina Christiana* 3). That is why people often argue about what a given passage of Scripture means.

Furthermore, the literal sense is not necessarily a historical sense because not every passage of Scripture is written in the genre of history. Some are historical, to be sure, and for those passages the literal sense is historical. But others are in the genre of law, or liturgy, or poetry, or exhortation, of song, or of any one of a number of other genres. For those passages, the literal sense is the principal meaning in terms of the genre's form of literary expression (CCC 110).

The other intended meanings are what the tradition calls "spiritual senses" (CCC 117). The spiritual senses are extensions of the literal sense. They take the literal sense and refer it to other things that God wants to say to us. There are three main spiritual senses:

1. The allegorical sense teaches us about Christ and his Church.
2. The tropological sense teaches us about how we should live our lives.
3. The anagogical sense teaches us about the union of our souls with God now and in eternity.

Once we know the literal sense of a passage, how can we come to know its spiritual meanings? The spiritual meaning of Sacred Scripture has been teased out by holy men and women for two millennia. That's not to say that the saints of ages past have pondered everything there is or ever will be to ponder in the Scriptures—the Scriptures contain an infinite amount of wisdom that no human person nor all of us put together could ever exhaust—but it is to say that the Magisterium of the Church has established some normative criteria of which we need to be aware. These criteria can be found in the Decrees on Scripture from the Council of Trent (DH 1507) and in the Dogmatic Constitution on the Catholic Faith, *Dei Filius*, from Vatican I (DH 3007).

The first rule is the rule of faith (CCC 114-15). The rule of faith states that we should interpret any given passage of Scripture according to the faith of the Church because all Scripture is inspired by the Holy Spirit, and it is that same Spirit that guides the Church into all truth. St. Augustine, an early formulator of this rule (*De doctrina Christiana* 2.2.2), annexes to it the rule of charity: when interpreting the Scriptures according to the rule of faith, we should always seek those meanings that build up our love of God and of our neighbor. Since we know that the fulfillment of those two greatest commandments is God's intention for us, we know that when we interpret the Sacred Scriptures according to them, we will be acting in accord with God's intention (*De doctrina Christiana* 3.10.15-16).

The second rule is the rule of the Fathers. It states that, as we are interpreting Scripture according to the rule of faith, we should never interpret Scripture contrary to the unanimous consent of the Church Fathers. The reason for this is that the Church Fathers are among the primary vehicles through which the Tradition of the Faith has been passed down to subsequent generations.

> *Interpretation of the inspired Scripture must be attentive above all to what God wants to reveal through the sacred authors for our salvation. What comes from the Spirit is not fully "understood except for the Spirit's action". (CCC 137)*

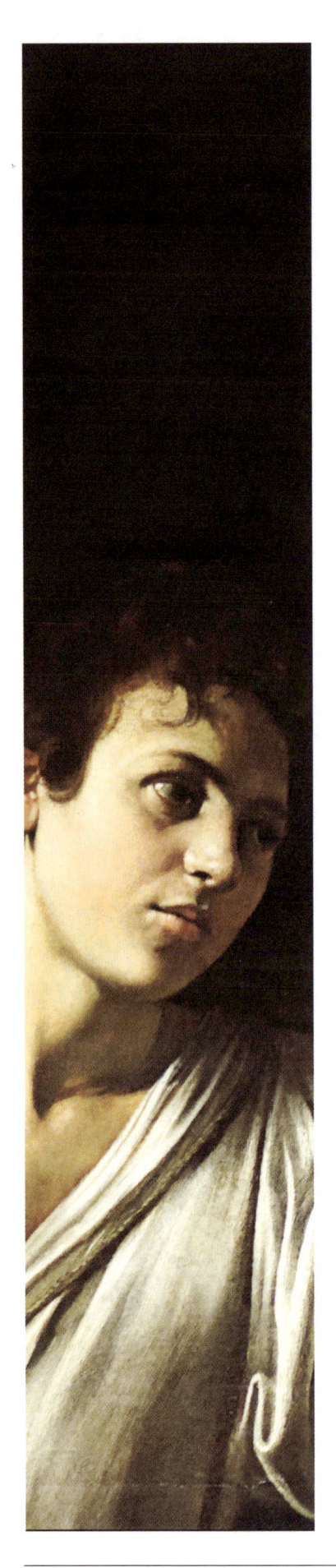

So how can we put all this together? Bishop Barron gives us the example of David. In the literal sense, whoever wrote 1-2 Samuel was thinking of David as a historical king. David lived in the eleventh century BC, united the disparate Israelite tribes, and established the capital of the Israelite kingdom in Jerusalem. But whoever wrote 1–2 Samuel was also open to what God might want to say to us by the life of David that he was narrating.

In the allegorical sense, David was a figure of Christ because he teaches us about who Christ is and prefigures it to a certain extent—David brought all Israel into one people, and Christ brings all nations into one people; David was given a never-ending royal line, and Christ was given a never-ending royal throne. In the tropological sense, David teaches us how we should act because he placed his covenant with God at the center of his life; he led others to it; and, when he sinned against God, he repented with a contrite heart. In the anagogical sense, David teaches us how to seek union with God in the total consecration of himself and his people to the will of the Lord. If we don't know who David is literally, we'll never know what David can teach us about Jesus, our lives, and our ultimate perfection in God; so likewise if we don't know the human meaning or literal sense of a passage, we'll never come authentically to its divine meaning.

In light of the four senses, the full richness of Scripture begins to come alive for us. The people of the Old Testament, though belonging to a distant place and time, are brought near to us as we learn about their history. Also, their history points us towards and participates in the history of our own salvation. As Bishop Barron sums it up, when we read 1-2 Samuel, our purpose "is to look at David and the figures around him precisely to understand Christ more fully."

†

HANNAH AND THE LAW OF THE GIFT

If our purpose in reading 1-2 Samuel is to understand Christ more fully, and if in the New Testament we first come to Christ through Mary, then it is fitting that as we approach the various figures of Christ presented to us in the story of David, we begin with one figure of Mary—Hannah (CCC 64).

10 ©2017 Word on Fire Catholic Ministries

In the literal sense of 1 Samuel 1-2, Hannah, whose name means, "[God] has shown favor," is one of the wives of Elkanah, and she is unable to bear children. Hannah is mercilessly teased by his other wife, Peninnah, because of her barrenness. One year, while in Shiloh to offer the yearly sacrifice, Hannah was worshipping at the tabernacle when the high priest, Eli, mistakes her for an alcoholic. She explains that she is entirely sober and that she has been praying for deliverance from her barrenness. Eli intercedes for her and she conceives and bears a son, Samuel, whose name may mean "God has heard." Thereafter, she sings a song praising and exulting the Lord for raising her up from lowliness and for putting down Peninnah's pride. Her song anticipates many of the exact words that Mary sings in the Magnificat. Hannah then consecrates Samuel to the Lord and to the Temple as a Nazirite.

A Nazirite is someone who is dedicated to the Lord for a certain period of time, during which he or she abstains from alcohol and from cutting his or her hair (Num 6:1-20). Nazirites observed the same ascetical disciplines as priests (Lev 10:9) and Levites (Ezek 44:20-21) when they went into the sanctuary to offer sacrifice. Nazirites were like priests who continually offered a sacrifice of their lives to God.

In the allegorical sense, Hannah's physical barrenness represents the spiritual barrenness of Israel as it awaits the Savior. Hannah's prayer, mistaken for drunkenness, represents her being full of the Holy Spirit as Mary was. In fact, the mistaking of spiritual fullness for drunkenness is a theme in Scripture; people made the same mistake about the Apostles on the day they were filled with the Holy Spirit at Pentecost (Acts 2:13). Hannah's offering of Samuel to the Lord as a Nazirite represents Mary's offering of Jesus as a sacrifice to God the Father. Just as Hannah offered Samuel in such a way that Samuel's life became a sacrifice, so when Mary learned that "you yourself a sword shall pierce" (Luke 2:35), she offered herself as a sacrifice united to her Son, whose whole life would be offered to God on the cross.

As Bishop Barron notes, the deepest union between Hannah and Mary is evident in the songs that each holy woman sings. These songs describe the pattern according to which God's gracious action unfolds in history. They begin with praise: "My heart exults in the Lord," says Hannah; "My soul magnifies the Lord," says Mary. They continue with an acknowledgement of their humility before God and their need for him. "My strength is exalted in the Lord," says Hannah; "He has looked with favor on his lowly servant," says Mary. They then describe that what has happened to them is a microcosm of the entire pattern by which God relates to humanity: putting down the mighty, exalting the lowly, filling the hungry, making the poor rich. Each woman sees in herself a figure of God's love for his entire people, even as she prepares to raise a son who will bear concrete witness to God's mercy. On account of Hannah's sacrifice, Samuel will grow up as a prophet, priest, and ruler of Israel—moreover, he will anoint the paradigmatic King of Israel, David. On account of Mary's sacrifice, Jesus will grow up as the fulfillment of all prophecy, priesthood, and kingship, as the *Messiah*, the anointed one of God.

In the tropological sense, Bishop Barron shows us how this Marian paradigm gives us a law according to which God governs the entire metaphysical and moral order: the law of the gift. "The law of the gift," Bishop Barron explains, "is a metaphysical and spiritual principle, and it runs like this: your being increases in the measure that you give it away." That principle is operative throughout the story of Hannah. The more Hannah gives herself away, the more she gives herself to the Lord in prayer, the more she offers up her much-desired son to the Lord through the Nazirite vow, the more she receives. This law is fulfilled in the person of Mary, who gives so completely of herself that she rightfully prophesies that she will be called "blessed" throughout all ages. Every time we say a "Hail Mary," that prophecy comes true, and we affirm the law of the gift whereby God calls each and every one of us to live according to the pattern of these holy women of God. And so, in the anagogical sense, every time we give ourselves away as a sacrifice to the Lord, we enter into a greater share of the divine life that Hannah anticipated and that Mary brought into the world.

THE STORY OF RUTH

Another figure of Mary who predates Hannah is Ruth. As Bishop Barron observes, Ruth seems to interrupt the long, sweeping, and male historical narrative that goes from Joshua to 2 Kings with a short, personal anecdote. But, as Bishop Barron also mentions, if we pay close attention to Ruth, we find that she and her life are packed with theological significance.

In the literal sense, the story of Ruth is quite simple. There is a famine in Israel, and an Israelite named Elimelech travels from his home in Bethlehem with his wife, Naomi, and two sons to a foreign land, Moab, whose people worship foreign gods, to find food. While they are there, Elimelech dies, and his two sons marry two foreigners, Orpah and Ruth. They settle in for a decade, and then the two sons die. This leaves Naomi, Orpah, and Ruth destitute—no father, no husband, and no children. As Bishop Barron points out, a woman without a child was about as low in social status as one could get at that time. A woman without a husband or father, the Book of Ruth tells us, was not only destitute, but in constant danger of sexual violence.

After all this calamity, Naomi hears that the Lord has given food to the Israelites, so she starts off to go home to Bethlehem. But she fears that Orpah and Ruth—being foreigners—won't be able to find a husband among the Israelites, and so will remain childless and destitute. Out of concern for their temporal welfare, she sends them back home to Moab. But going back home does not just mean returning to the house they had lived in for a decade. Without an Israelite husband, it also means return to the worship of foreign gods. Orpah gives Naomi a kiss goodbye and goes back to her gods. Ruth, on the other hand, clings to Naomi and to the Lord. Naomi and Ruth then return to Bethlehem, together.

Here is where the story takes an unexpected turn. According to Deuteronomy 25:5-6, a deceased husband's brother has the duty to marry his brother's wife and to father children with her in his brother's name. This is called a "levirite" marriage. In the process of searching for food, Ruth runs into someone who happens to be one such kinsman, Boaz. The only trouble is that Boaz is not the immediate next of kin. Boaz therefore justly informs the next of kin of Ruth's situation and of the levirite duty. The next of kin, realizing that this would mean partitioning the inheritance due his children with the children of Ruth, rejects the levirite marriage, and thus the right passes to Boaz. Boaz subsequently marries Ruth and they have a son, Obed, who is the grandfather of David.

In the allegorical sense, the story of Ruth is the story of Mary. Naomi represents the land of Israel, and Elimelech, whose name means "My God is King," represents Israel's covenantal relationship with God. Elimelech's death represents the breaking of the covenant, when Israel no longer sees God as its king. That is the deeper meaning of the phrase that Bishop Barron quotes from the end of Judges, "In those days there was no king in Israel; everyone did what he thought best." The death of Elimelech's sons represents the Deuteronomic curse, the loss of the blessings that depended on the covenant. Orpah and Ruth represent the two kingdoms: Orpah represents the Kingdom of Israel, and Ruth represents the Kingdom of Judah. The Kingdom of Israel turns away from God and so departs from the land of Israel into the Assyrian Captivity. The Kingdom of Judah clings to the land and to God, and so returns after the Babylonian Captivity.

Here again is where things get interesting. Boaz's next of kin represents Satan. With the death of the people's relationship with God, Satan has dominion over them. Thus even after Judah returns from captivity, it is not spiritually fruitful because it is still in bondage to sin. But Satan's lack of love for the people is his ultimate undoing. Boaz represents Christ. He is a just man who by his love for the people redeems them from bondage to Satan and makes them fruitful once more. That makes Ruth the first-redeemed, the first-restored to fruitfulness when the people stray from the covenant. And it is through this figure of Mary that we receive David, the forefather of the Savior.

DAVID THE KING

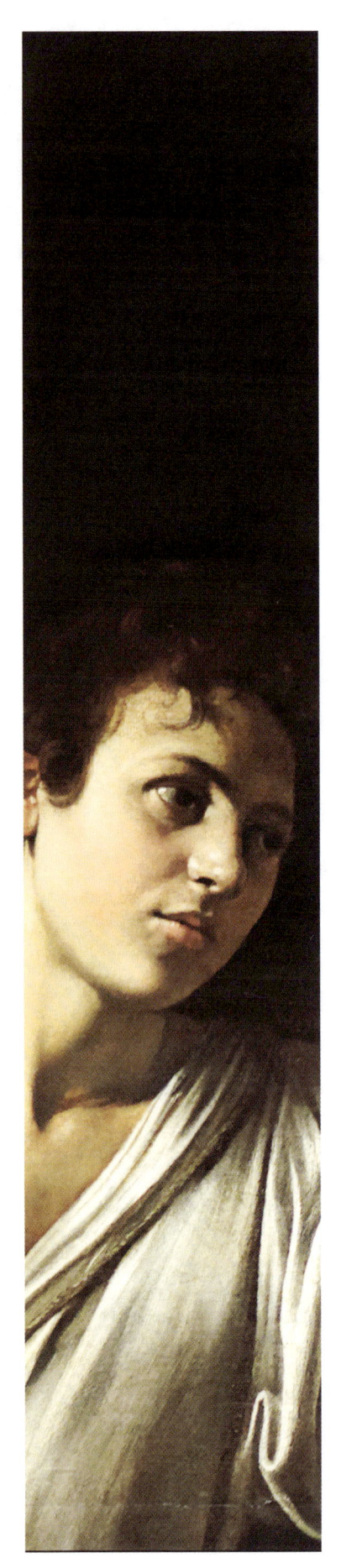

QUESTIONS FOR UNDERSTANDING

1. What human and spiritual insights can we gain by understanding the authorship of 1-2 Samuel? (CCC 109-114)

2. Summarize the literal and spiritual meanings of the story of Hannah (1 Sam 1:1-28; 1 Sam 17:37-51; CCC 115-119).

3. How does the story of Hannah serve as an allegory of Mary?

4. What is the "law of the gift"? Give some examples from Scripture and your own life to illustrate this law.

QUESTIONS FOR APPLICATION

1. Pick a biblical woman, Ruth or Hannah. How does the pattern of her physical life relate to events that have happened in your life of faith?

2. How does living according to the "law of the gift" compare with the societal "law" or attitudes in your local community? What challenges you most about the differences between the two "laws"?

3. Write your own song of praise and gratitude using Hannah's song as an example (1 Samuel 2:1-10).

DAVID THE KING

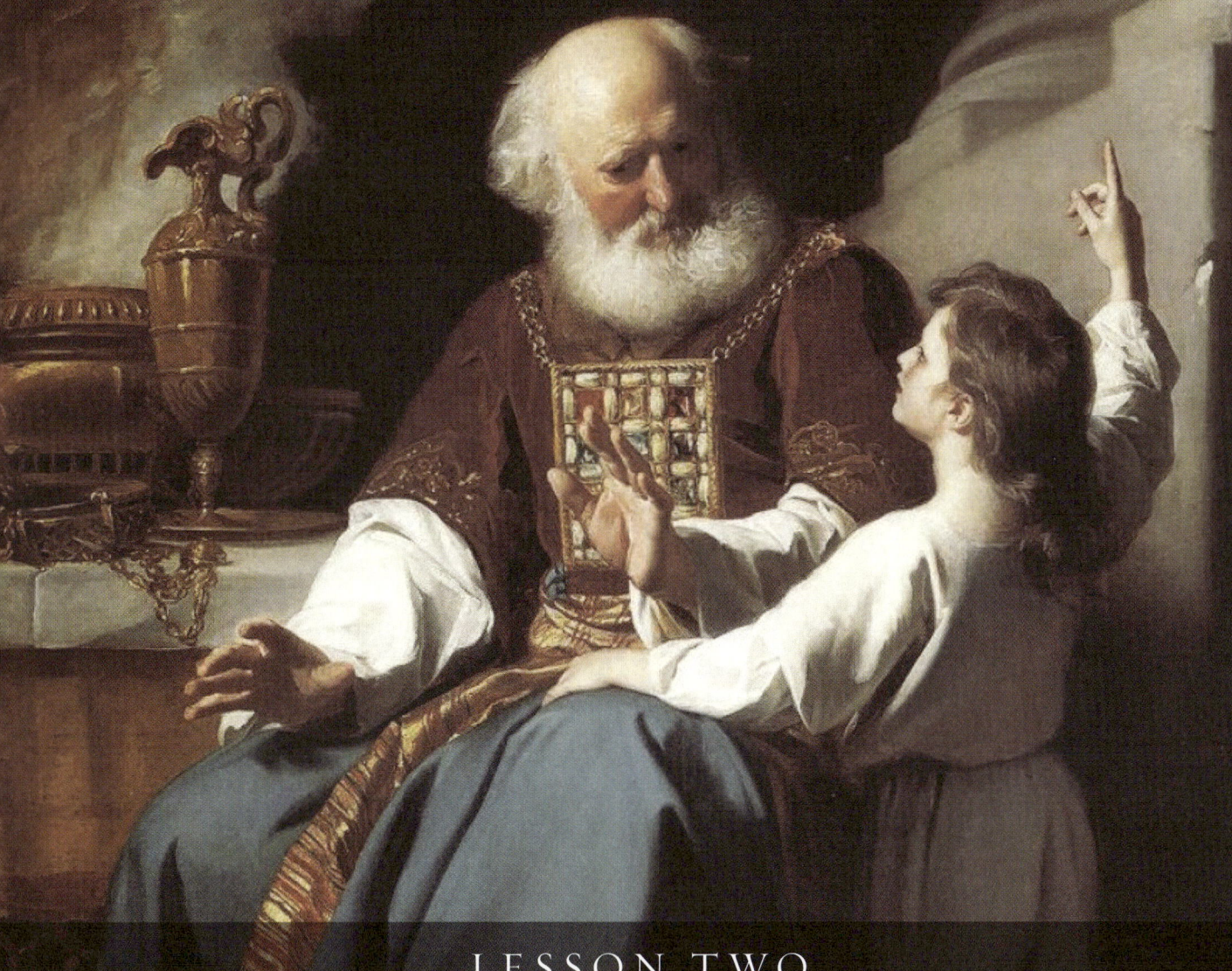

LESSON TWO
YOUR SERVANT IS LISTENING

LESSON TWO IMAGE

Samuel Reading to Eli the Judgments of God Upon Eli's House. John Singleton Copley, 1780. Hartford, Connecticut. Wadsworth Atheneum.

YOUR SERVANT IS LISTENING

LESSON TWO OUTLINE

I. ELI THE HIGH PRIEST'S DISASTROUS RULE
   A. Eli raised Samuel in the Temple
   B. Eli's sons carried out priestly roles, yet were very sinful
   C. The people complained to Eli and he gave his sons a small reprimand but did not act forcefully to stop their sinfulness
   D. Trouble comes from kings not taking or exercising their power

II. CALL OF SAMUEL
   A. During this time, "the word of the Lord was scarce and visions infrequent" because Israel wasn't listening
   B. Eli doesn't see physically and spiritually; does not lead according to his role as judge, prophet, and high priest
   C. Eli finally realizes the Lord is calling Samuel and tells him to say, "Speak, Lord, your servant is listening."
   D. God tells Samuel what retributions will come from Eli's failure to stop his sons' sinful behavior
      1. Philistines defeat Israel and whole army is wiped out
      2. Eli's sons are killed in battle
      3. When Eli hears of their death, he falls, breaks his neck, and dies

III. PARALLEL TO CHURCH'S SEX SCANDAL
   A. Scandal and woe came to Israel and to the contemporary Church (the new Israel) when the sinful behavior of priests was not stopped or corrected by Church leaders
   B. Word of God was still being preached at these times, but ignored
   C. God delivers retribution out of love for Israel and for the Church. God hands Israel and the Church over to its enemies (Philistines and secular culture respectively) during time of purification.

DAVID THE KING

IV. GOD DOES NOT ABANDON ISRAEL OR THE CHURCH
   A. Stirs up the heart of Hannah who conceives Samuel—redemptive prophet and king for Israel
   B. Raises up new priests today to be part of the solution

LESSON TWO
YOUR SERVANT IS LISTENING

In the previous talk, Bishop Barron introduced us to two people, Ruth and Hannah, whose Marian lives show us what it means to live according to the law of the gift. In this talk, he introduces us to the personal and social consequences of refusing to live that way through the story of Eli and his two sons, Phinehas and Hophni.

THE ISRAELITE PRIESTHOOD

In the literal sense, we are told that Eli is a priest of God at Shiloh. At this time in Israel's history Shiloh is roughly analogous to what Jerusalem will later become: it is the center of Israelite life and worship, the place where they offer the sacrifices to God as part of their covenant with him.

The central features of Israelite worship were all located at the tabernacle in Shiloh. The tabernacle, which God commanded the Israelites to make in Exodus 26, was a sort of mobile tent-sanctuary, made of fancy cloths and gilded fixtures, which served the needs of the Israelites for a place in which to worship the Lord until the building of temple under the reign of King David's son, Solomon.

Inside the tabernacle was the Ark of the Covenant (Exod 25:10-22). The Ark of the Covenant was a gilded container, carried about in the camp of Israel, which housed three artifacts from the events wherein God revealed himself to his people: Aaron's staff, manna from the wilderness, and the tablets of the Law (Heb 9:4). The Ark of the Covenant lived behind a veil in the center of the tabernacle, which was called the Holy of Holies, and represented the presence of the Lord among his people (Exod 26:34).

Originally, the sacrificial cult of Israel was rather simple. Every day at morning and at evening they were to offer a lamb on the altar for burnt offerings on behalf of all the people (Exod 29:38-46; Num 28:1-8). In addition, there were three large annual festivals (Exod 23:14-19), and a small variety of other sacrifices. (Exod 20:24-25). These sacrifices were performed by priests who inherited their roles. The Book of Exodus summarizes the role of priests in three points: they were to be "holy to the Lord," (Exod 28:36), to intercede for the good of Israel (Exod 28:29), and to do penance and thereby make atonement for the sins of Israel (Exod 28:30, 38). They were assisted by the firstborn of all the families of Israel (Exod 2:29; Num 3:45).

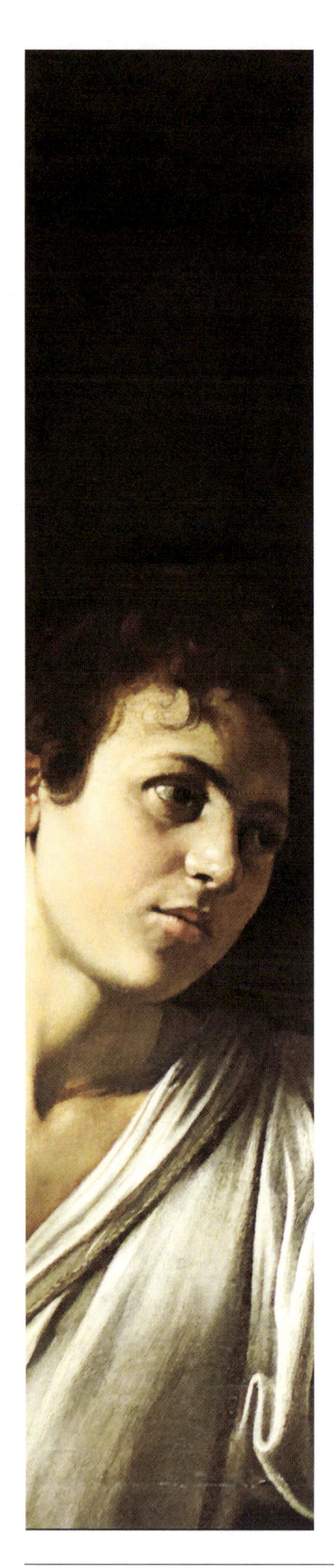

Just as Aaron, Moses's brother, had ministered to Moses during the Exodus, so likewise Aaron and his sons were set apart to minister to the people of Israel as its priests (Exod 28:1-2). Aaron had four sons who offered "unholy fire" and were struck dead by the Lord (Lev 10:1-3); they died early without sons, and Aaron's successors were therefore drawn from the houses of his other two sons, Eleazar and Ithamar (Num 3:4, 26:61; 1 Chron 24:2-3).

The simplicity of the sacrificial cult did not last for long. Immediately after the ratification of the covenant, while Moses was on the mountain with God, Aaron led the people into sin by breaking the very first commandment: they worshipped a golden calf (Exod 32). This failure led to a significant change. When Moses saw the people running amok after the establishment of the Golden Calf, Moses asked the people who would join him in fidelity to the Lord. The tribe of Levi rallied to his side and executed judgment upon the other tribes. As a reward, all the male Levites who were not descended from Aaron were set aside for a special priestly ministry at the service of the sons of Aaron, replacing the firstborn of all the families of Israel (Exod 32:25-29; Num 3:45, 8:16). They did not perform the sacrifices themselves, but they did assist the sons of Aaron with the sacrifices (Num 18:1-7).

A second instance of idolatry led to a second change in the priesthood. At a time when the Israelites were dwelling among the Moabites—the same people from whom Orpah and Ruth later came—an Israelite by the name of Zimri married a foreigner by the name of Cozbi. In order to prevent Israel from turning away from the Marian pattern of Ruth towards the idolatrous pattern of Orpah, Eleazar's son, Phinehas (not to be confused with Eli's son of the same name), put the two of them to death. As a reward for his zeal, God promised that the sons of Phinehas would possess the high priesthood in perpetuity (Num 25:10-13). That God did not make such a promise to anyone among the sons of Ithamar foreshadows what will later happen to Eli, who was from the house of Ithamar.

The sacrifices themselves also underwent significant development after the period of the Golden Calf. In addition to the daily offerings, there were specifications for weekly and monthly offerings, as well as more elaborate specifications for holiday offerings (Num 28-29). The small variety of other sacrifice became a highly specified system: burnt offerings, cereal offerings, peace offerings (both thanksgiving and votive), sin offerings, and guilt offerings (Lev 1-7), ordination offerings (Lev 8), purification offerings (Lev 12-15), and—once per year—an offering of atonement made by the high priest himself in the Holy of Holies for all the sins of Israel (Lev 16).

THE SUPPORT OF ISRAELITE PRIESTS

Generally speaking, the priests were extremely well provided for in the sacrificial cult of Israel. If we simply take the first five main offerings mentioned in Leviticus, we find that in only one case—the whole burnt offering—was the entire sacrificial victim lost in the sacrifice, and in only two other cases—a sin offering when the priest was implicated in the sin, or a thanksgiving offering when the priest was thanking God for his ordination—was the priest not permitted to eat of it at all. Below is a description of the other offerings:

Cereal Offerings

- What is offered: Fine flour, oil, frankincense, salt (Lev 2:1, 13)
- What is devoted to God: All the frankincense, and a handful of flour, oil, and salt (Lev 2:2)
- What is devoted to the priest: All the rest of the flour, oil, and salt (Lev 6:16-18; 7:9-10)

Peace Offerings

  A. Thanksgiving Offerings

- What is offered: A male or female ox, lamb, or goat without blemish (Lev 3:1), unleavened cakes mixed with oil, unleavened wafers spread with oil, cakes of fine flour mixed with oil (Lev 7:12)
- What is devoted to God: The kidneys, the lobe of the liver, the blood, and the fat of the animal, and one of each kind of baked good (Lev 3:3-4, 17)
- What is devoted to the priest: The breast and right thigh of the animal (Lev 7:21-36) and one of each kind of baked good (Lev 7:14)
- What is devoted to the people: The rest of the animal

DAVID THE KING

B. Votive Offerings

- What is offered: A male or female ox, lamb, or goat without blemish (Lev 3:1)

- What is devoted to God: The kidneys, the lobe of the liver, the blood, and the fat of the animal (Lev 3:3-4, 17)

- What is devoted to the priest: The breast and right thigh of the animal (Lev 7:21-36)

- What is devoted to the people: The rest of the animal

Sin Offerings

A. Sins of Rulers (Sins involving a priest, whether alone or with the rest of Israel, are treated first and are more serious)

- What is offered: A male goat without blemish (Lev 4:23)

- What is devoted to God: The fat and the blood (Lev 4:25-26)

- What is devoted to the priest: The rest of the animal (Lev 7:26)

B. Sins of Common People

- What is offered: A female goat or lamb without blemish (Lev 4:28, 32)

- What is devoted to God: The fat and the blood (Lev 4:30-31, 34-35)

- What is devoted to the priest: The rest of the animal (Lev 7:26)

C. Sins of the Poor

- What is offered: Two turtledoves or two young pigeons (Lev 5:7)

- What is devoted to God: The whole of one, and the blood of the other (Lev 5:8-9)

- What is devoted to the priest: The second bird (Lev 7:26)

D. Sins of the Destitute

- What is offered: 1/10 of an ephah of fine flour—about 9 cups (Lev 5:11)

- What is devoted to God: A handful of the fine flour (Lev 5:12)

- What is devoted to the priest: The rest of the flour—about a half gallon (Lev 5:13)

Guilt Offerings
- What is offered: A male sheep without blemish (Lev 5:15, 18; 6:6)
- What is devoted to God: The kidneys, the lobe of the liver, the fat, and the blood (Lev 7:3-5)
- What is devoted to the priest: The rest of the animal (Lev 7:7-8)

In each of the aforementioned sacrifices, the priest receives a significant amount of food. In a cereal offering, whatever goes beyond the bare minimum; in a peace offering, the breast and right thigh of a female lamb or goat; in a thanksgiving offering, a variety of baked goods; in a sin offering for a ruler, all the meat from a male goat; in a sin offering for a common person, all the meat from a female lamb or goat; in a sin offering for a poor person, a turtledove or pigeon; in a sin offering for a destitute person, about half a gallon of fine flour; in a guilt offering, all the meat from a male sheep.

Moreover, while the consumption of blood had been forbidden since God first gave permission for his people to eat meat, since it represented the life of the animal (Gen 9:4), the laws introduced after the Golden Calf contain a universal prohibition on the consumption of fat as well (Lev 3:16-17). This new prohibition was followed by adopting the practice of boiling meat after it was sacrificed rather than roasting it (Lev 6:28, 8:31; Num 6:19). The reason for this is simple: boiling renders the fat out of the meat, while roasting cooks the fat into the meat. Prior to the Golden Calf, on at least one occasion—the first Passover—Israel had been commanded to roast the sacrificial victim and not to boil it (Exod 12:8-9); after the Golden Calf, God commands that even the Passover be boiled (Deut 16:7).

These changes gave way to the structure of the priesthood as it existed under Eli. To summarize, all priests were led by the high priests, who were patrilineal descendants of Aaron, either through Eleazar or through Ithamar. High priests were assisted in the offering of sacrifice by the other male descendants of Aaron; Aaronic priests were assisted by the other male members of the tribe of Levi. All together, the priests provided for the people by carrying out Israel's sacrificial cult, in which the blood of animals was poured out, their fat was offered to God, and the priests and people—as appropriate for a given sacrifice—boiled the sacrificial victim and ate of it.

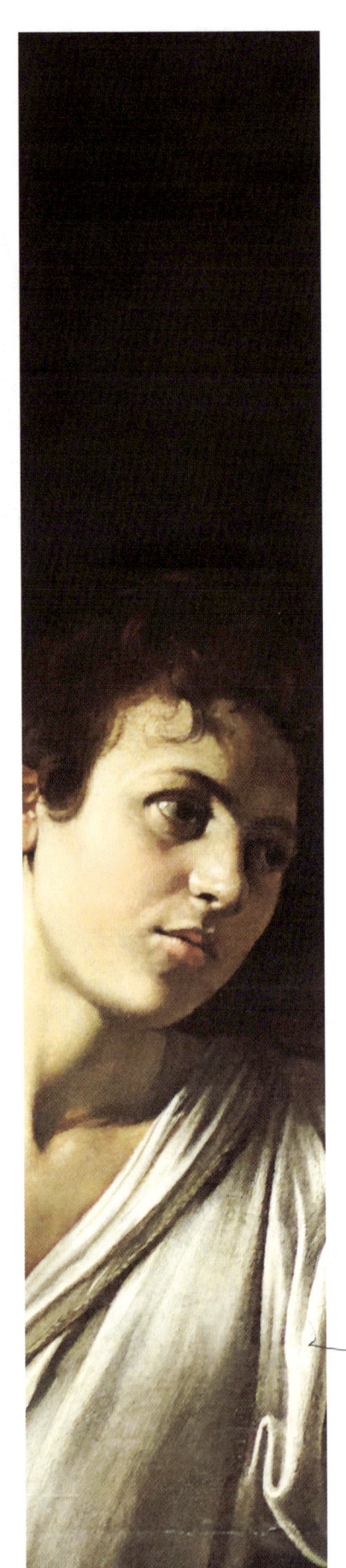

ELI, PHINEHAS, AND HOPHNI: THE FAILURE OF THE PRIESTS

We are now in a position to understand what Scripture says in the literal sense about Eli, Phinehas, and Hophni. Eli was a high priest at Shiloh. He was a descendent of Aaron through Ithamar. This means that Eli was not among the sons of the other Phinehas, the one to whose descendants God promised a perpetual priesthood. This alone should tell us that something is not quite right with Eli. Moreover, Eli's two sons, Phinehas and Hophni, were Aaronide priests who were charged with offering sacrifice under the auspices of Eli. We are told right from the start that they "were worthless men; they had no regard for the Lord" (1 Sam 2:12). We then get a list of their offenses against the sacrificial cult of the Lord.

If we want to understand what comes next, we have to place the sacrifice described in context. Since Scripture tells us that the people, rather than the priest, were boiling the meat (1 Sam 2:13-14), we can deduce that it is speaking of a peace offering, because this is the only regular sacrifice in which a portion of the meat was deliberately set aside for the people. Since we know that this was a peace offering, we can compare the actions of Phinehas and Hophni to the laws prescribed for peace offerings. In a peace offering, a male or female ox, lamb, or goat was sacrificed, and the breast and thigh of the animal was reserved for the priest. The priest and people would then take their respective portions of the sacrificial victim and boil them. After boiling, they would eat their respective portions.

First Offense

The first offense of Phinehas and Hophni was stealing from the people's food. We are told that:

> When someone offered a sacrifice, the priest's servant would come with a three-pronged fork, while the meat was still boiling, and would thrust it into the basin, kettle, caldron, or pot. Whatever the fork brought up, the priest would take for himself. (1 Sam 2:13-14)

©2017 Word on Fire Catholic Ministries

Let us call to mind that in almost every sacrifice, the priest was the only person who got to eat anything. A peace offering was one of the only times that the person offering the sacrifice got to eat of it, and even then, the breast and the right thigh were reserved for the priest. To picture this concretely, we can consider that the average lamb is roughly 100 lbs. when slaughtered. Typically only 50% of a lamb is edible. That leaves about 50 lbs. of bone-in meat per lamb. Of that 50 lbs., the breast and right thigh account for about a third, which in this case is about 17 lbs.

Phinehas and Hophni, dissatisfied with the fact that they had just gotten over 15 lbs. of organic, grass-fed lamb, went back to the people who had offered the lamb, stuck a fork in the pot, and took whatever came out. Presumably the fork was large enough that they could manage to steal another complete cut from the lamb, drastically reducing the amount that the people got to eat. This was a twofold sin: it was a sin against God, in that it represented a drastic abuse of the sacrificial cult of the Lord; and it was a sin against those who came to worship the Lord, because it scandalized them and involved stealing food that lawfully belonged to them.

Second Offense

The second offense of Phinehas and Hophni is demanding raw meat before the sacrifice. We are told that:

> In fact, even before the fat was burned, the priest's servant would come and say to the one offering the sacrifice, "Give me some meat to roast for the priest. He will not accept boiled meat from you, only raw meat." And if this one protested, "Let the fat be burned first, then take whatever you wish," he would reply, "No, give it to me now, or else I will take it by force." (1 Sam 2:15-16)

This is actually a triple offense. The first part of the offense is that the priests are demanding that the people offer them meat before the fat was burned. That is a direct violation of the law for peace offerings, which stipulates that the kidneys, the lobe of the liver, and the fat all be burned. The reason that they wanted the meat with the fat still on it was to commit the other part of the offense: roasting the meat. They wanted more fat on the meat so that when they roasted it, all that fat would cook into the meat rather than being boiled out of it. This was in violation of the prohibition of eating animal fat after the Golden Calf. The final sin was scandalizing and stealing from the people who came to worship the Lord.

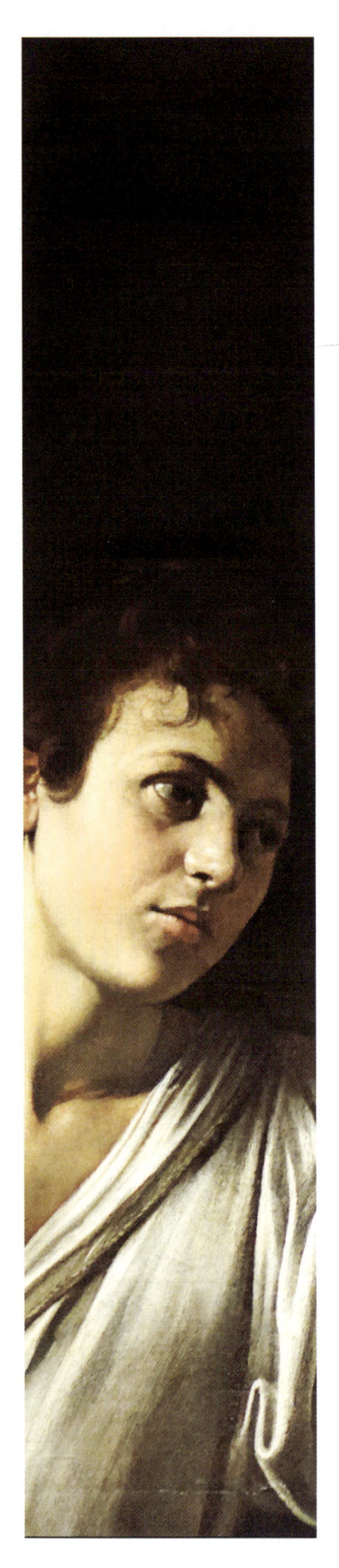

Third Offense

We only learn about the third offense of Phinehas and Hophni in passing. "Now Eli was very old, and he heard all that his sons were doing to all Israel, and how they lay with the women who served at the entrance to the tent of meeting" (1 Sam 2:22). So, if all the manifold abuses of the peace offering were not enough, Phinehas and Hophni are committing fornication and/or adultery (at best) or rape (at worst) with the women who served at the door to the tent of meeting. This was a grave sin against the women themselves, but it was also, as Bishop Barron notes, a grave sin against anyone who would come to worship there.

The Response

Eli's response points to the real source of the problem: Eli had effectively given up on his priestly and kingly ministry.

> So he said to them: "Why are you doing such things? I hear from everyone that your behavior is depraved. Stop this, my sons! The report that I hear the LORD's people spreading is not good. If someone sins against another, anyone can intercede for the sinner with the LORD; but if anyone sins against the LORD, who can intercede for the sinner?" But they disregarded their father's warning, since the LORD wanted them dead. (1 Sam 2:23-25)

Let us consider his first phrase: "If someone sins against another, anyone can intercede for the sinner." Eli clearly has his sons' sins of theft and adultery in mind here. Theft and adultery were grave offenses against the Ten Commandments, each of which incurred grave obligations under the Mosaic Law. Theft required that the guilty party make restitution plus twenty percent; it also required a guilt offering in which the priest was said to make atonement for the sin (Lev 5:20-26). By saying that "anyone can intercede," Eli is abdicating his own high priestly role of mediating for his sons. Adultery, on the other hand, was a capital offense (Lev 18:20; 20:10), except in the case of a slave women (Lev 19:20). Eli was further abdicating his high priestly role by not taking action against his adulterous sons.

Now let us consider the second phrase, "if anyone sins against the Lord, who can intercede for the sinner?" This phrase represents the abdication of Eli's priestly ministry even more than the first. For, in addition to the law of sin offering and guilt offerings for various offenses, it was the high priest alone who could make a more complete atonement for the sins of Israel on the Day of Atonement (Lev 16). In essence, Eli's warning against his sons can be reduced to something like this: "That's really bad, but I'm not really going to do anything about it. I'm not even going to make atonement for you, because I don't really believe in this stuff anymore."

The Judgement

After Eli's ineffective response, a man of God arrives to proclaim judgment upon Eli and his sons (1 Sam 2:27-36). The judgment is harsh. The strength of Eli's house is to be cut off, every one of its members will die early, and they will be poor and destitute; they will be deprived of their priestly service so that they do not even get to eat what lawfully belongs to the priests. The sign of this is that both of Eli's sons will die on the same day. Eli's attitude remains nonchalant. After Samuel utters a similar warning in harsher terms (1 Sam 3:14), Eli responds: "It is the Lord. What is pleasing in the Lord's sight, the Lord will do." (1 Sam 3:18)

Traditionally, scholars point to Eli's failure as a father to account for his implication in his son's punishment. So the argument goes, a father has the duty to correct his sons when they err; Eli did not correct his errant sons; therefore Eli is at fault for their behavior. That is true, and the reason that most scholars point to this is that it is the most obvious reason given to us in Scripture (1 Sam 3:13).

Yet in addition to his failure to restrain his sons, if we read closely, we find out that Eli actually *joined in with his sons* in stealing meat, roasting it, and eating it. When the man of God comes to punish Eli, he addresses not Eli's sons but Eli directly and says: "Why... look with greedy eye at my sacrifices and my offerings which I commanded, and honor your sons above me by fattening yourselves upon the choicest parts of every offering of my people Israel?" (1 Sam 2:29). Notice that when the man of God speaks of "fattening yourselves," he does not distinguish between Eli and his sons. Indeed, Eli had been fattening himself along with them. He had grown to such proportions that when the man of God's word came true, and Eli heard that his sons had been struck down by Philistines (1 Sam 4:17), "Eli fell over backward from his seat by the side of the gate; and his neck was broken and he died, for he was an old man, *and heavy*" (1 Sam 4:18; emphasis added). There are no throwaway lines in Scripture. The coda of that sentence is supposed to remind us that people don't ordinarily break their necks when they fall out of chairs. Eli had grown so heavy along with his sons by disobeying the commandments of the Lord that he perished along with them.

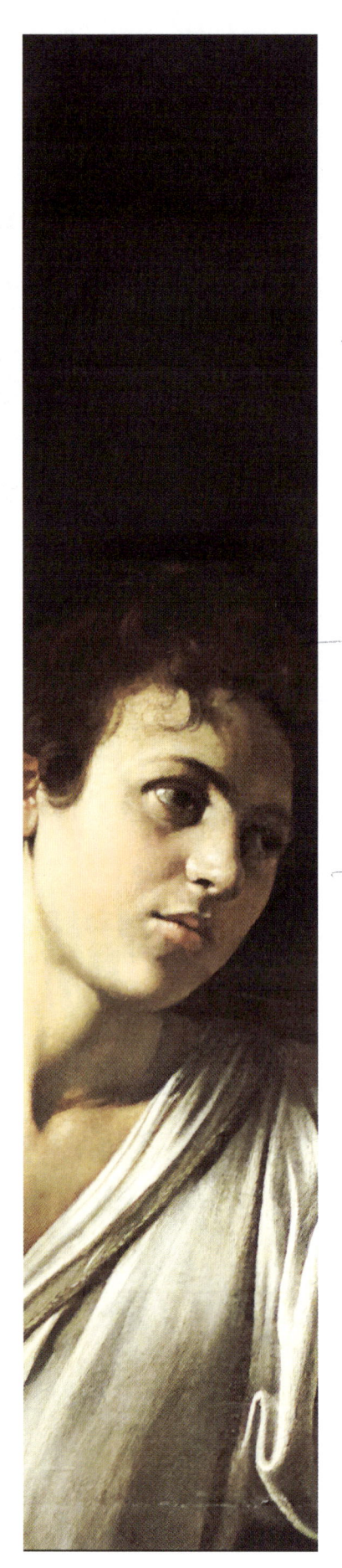

The Aftermath

Eli's apathy when confronted with his sin against the priesthood points to a further problem. If we read closely, we find out that Eli is not just the high priest. We read at the end of his life that he had been judge over Israel for forty years (1 Sam 4:18). After the conquest of Canaan and prior to the establishment of the kingship under Saul, the judges in Israel were the highest governing authority (Judg 2:11-23). This means that not only did Eli sin by laziness in failing at fatherly duties, he also sinned as Israel's ruler for failing to execute judgment upon his sons.

Eli's failures as judge take center stage after he receives his warnings from the man of God and from Samuel. We read that "Israel went out to battle against the Philistines" (1 Sam 4:1). Notice that it does not say that the Philistines attacked. The battle was Israel's choice, and as judge Eli was also Israel's commander-in-chief: it was Eli who gave the order to attack.

The first battle was a failure; Israel lost 4,000 men (1 Sam 4:2). Fearing a greater loss, the elders sent for the ark, because they believed that the Lord dwelt upon it (1 Sam 4:3). Eli acquiesces and sends the ark along with his sons, Phinehas and Hophni. Here we see the theme of the inactive king that Bishop Barron points to, on display in its fullest. Eli has given up his responsibility as judge just as much as he has given up his responsibility as high priest. A judge was supposed to lead the people in battle. That is what prior judges had done; it was, as it were, part of the job description. "Whenever the Lord raised up judges for them, the Lord was with the judge, and he saved them from the hand of their enemies all the days of the judge" (Judg 2:18). That was not to be the case this time. As Bishop Barron observes, God remained faithful to his promise to be there for his people, but since Eli and the people were no longer faithful to the Lord, they were no longer willing to receive his help.

Part of the help that the people were missing was guidance from the Lord as to what to do. As Bishop Barron highlights, that is not because God was not ready to guide his people. Bishop Barron quotes the narrator, explaining that "the word of the Lord was rare in those days; there was no frequent vision" (1 Sam 3:1), and points out that Eli himself had become physically blind as a symbol of Israel's spiritual blindness (1 Sam 3:2). This represents a third failure of Eli: his failure as a prophet. Eli is, as it were, the epitome of Israelite failure: failure as a priest, failure as a ruler, and failure as a prophet. This spelled disaster for the people of Israel when they marched on the Philistines a second time.

The estrangement of Eli from God and his failure at all three of his offices is made palpable by the journey of the ark into the battle. In any other circumstance, the presence of the ark should have spelled instant victory for the people. But not this time. The ark goes, Phinehas and Hophni go, the elders and the soldiers go, but Eli stays home. At least when the ark was in Shiloh and Eli stayed home, Eli stayed home with God. But when he acquiesces to the ark's departure, he consents to estrangement from God. Had Eli gone into battle, Israel would have been victorious, because God is always faithful to his promises and God had promised to work through the judges to bring victory to his people. But Eli was too heavy-set from feasting on stolen sacrifices, too weak from nepotism, too blind from closing his heart, to go. The result was an even more drastic failure. Without a priest-judge-prophet to lead them, 30,000 Israelites perish, and the Philistines capture the ark (1 Sam 4:10-11).

Eli's estrangement from God has lasting effects, in accordance with the prophecy made against Eli's house. The first thing that happens is that nearly all Eli's descendants are wiped out. A few generations later, when David's sons are rivaling for the throne and Solomon prevails, Solomon deposes the existing high priest descended from Eli's house—the house of Ithamar—as he had supported the kingly claim of his rival brother, Adonijah. He was the last priest from Eli's house to serve, thus ending the high priestly status of the house forever.

†

THE ALLEGORICAL AND TROPOLOGICAL SENSES

In the allegorical sense, the priesthood of the Old Testament looks forward to the priesthood of Jesus Christ and of his Church. The Book of Hebrews describes the connection.

> But when Christ came as high priest of the good things that have come to be, passing through the greater and more perfect tabernacle not made by hands,

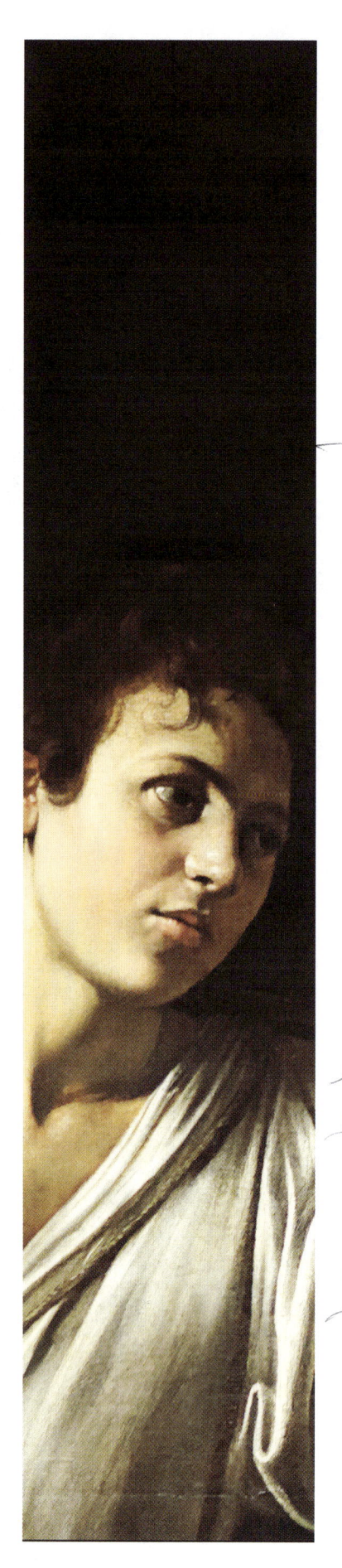

that is, not belonging to this creation, he entered once for all into the sanctuary, not with the blood of goats and calves but with his own blood, thus obtaining eternal redemption. For if the blood of goats and bulls and the sprinkling of a heifer's ashes can sanctify those who are defiled so that their flesh is cleansed, how much more will the blood of Christ, who through the eternal spirit offered himself unblemished to God, cleanse our consciences from dead works to worship the living God. (Heb 9:11-14)

The death of Christ on the cross fulfilled the expectations of every sacrifice of the Old Testament (CCC 614): a thanksgiving, votive, guilt, and sin offering all rolled into one whole burnt offering of himself, consumed by the burning fire of charity as he poured out his blood for us (CCC 613).

Beginning after the Resurrection, Christ gave to ordained men a sharing in his priesthood, modeled on the priesthood of the Old Testament. To the bishops, he gave a full sharing in his high priestly ministry. To the presbyters (priests), he gave a share in his ministry corresponding to the Aaronic priests. To the deacons, he gave a share in his ministry corresponding to the Levitical priests (CCC 1541-1543).

In the transition from the Old Testament priesthood to the New Testament priesthood, some things changed, and some things stayed the same. The two most significant things that have changed are the character of the office and the nature of the sacrifice. The character of the office has changed, because by the Sacrament of Holy Orders, the priest of the New Testament stands *in persona Christi*, in the person of Christ, performing God's action in the liturgy of the Church (CCC 1548). The nature of the sacrifice has changed because the sacrifices of the Mosaic Law, each of which prefigured the sacrifice of Jesus in some way, have been fulfilled in Jesus' sacrifice on the cross, which is made present to us in the Eucharist. The Eucharist, which means "thanksgiving," is the Christian fulfillment of the thanksgiving offering (CCC 1328). In the Old Testament, an unblemished lamb and cakes of fine flour were offered; in the New Testament, Jesus is the unblemished lamb who offers himself under the form of bread and wine on the altar at Mass (CCC 608, 1339).

The two most significant things that have stayed the same are the sacred nature of the priesthood and the temptations that face priests. The sacred nature of the priesthood has stayed the same, because it remains a calling whereby people are set apart as "holy to the Lord," so that they can serve as mediators for the people who are in a covenant relationship with the Lord. The temptations that face priests have stayed the same because human nature, wounded by sin after the Fall, has stayed the same.

Since the temptations that face priests have stayed the same, we can read the story of Eli, Phinehas, and Hophni in a tropological sense, pointing to the same dangers among New Testament priests as were faced by Old Testament priests. Briefly stated, those dangers are: financial impropriety, liturgical irreverence, sexual abuse, and laxity in the face of grave scandal.

Bishop Barron hones in on the latter two temptations, sexual abuse and laxity in the face of grave scandal, because these are the most well-publicized of scandalous behaviors among priests in recent years. The combination of the two created a "perfect storm" resulting in harm done directly to thousands of lay faithful, and scandal caused indirectly throughout the Church and throughout the world. But in essence, all four share the same root—they occur when someone who has been called by God to be "holy to the Lord" (Exod 28:36), to intercede for the good of the faithful (Exod 28:29), and to do penance and thereby make atonement for the sins of faithful (Exod 28:30, 38), seeks his own good rather than the good of those entrusted to his care. At that point he faces the temptation to turn the goods of others towards his own benefit, the worship of God towards his own glory, the dignity of others towards his own pleasure, and to exchange the virtue of others for his own complacency. Any time these things happen—and they do happen—it causes direct harm to the people who suffer them and indirect harm to countless others through scandal. It also harms the priest himself and jeopardizes the continued fulfillment of his sacred ministry.

Yet we should not lose hope. As Bishop Barron reminds us, God is always at work, even in the darkest of times. And just as God was still with the Church, sending her vocations to transform it in the midst of the sexual abuse scandal, as Bishop Barron recounts, so likewise was he at work in time of Eli, Phinehas, and Hophni, raising up a priestly, prophetic, and judicial vocation in Samuel to do the will of the Lord and to transform the people of Israel into something yet more glorious than they had ever been.

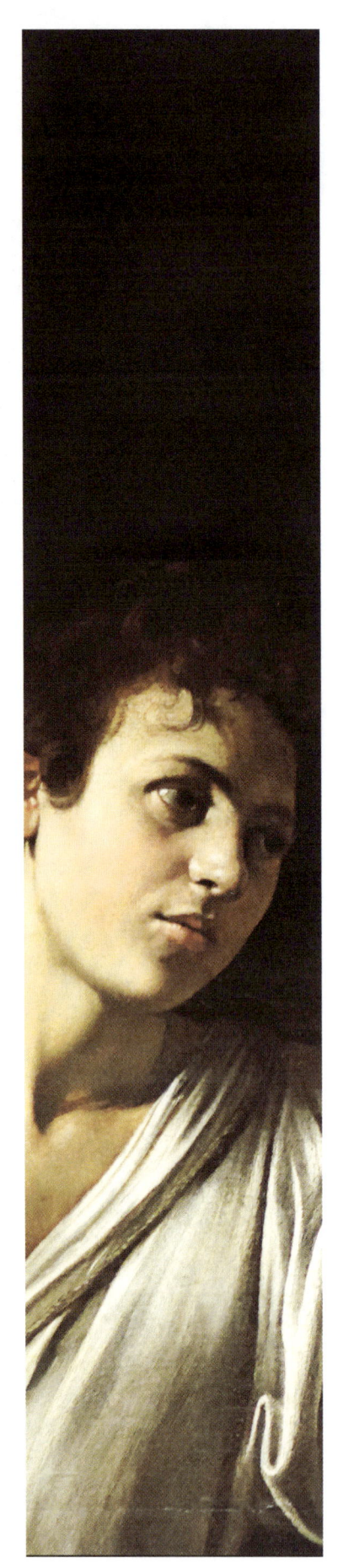

QUESTIONS FOR UNDERSTANDING

1. What were the three ways in which Phinehas and Hophni sinned against the Lord? (1 Sam 2:12-17, 22)

2. In what ways did Eli fail to fulfill his role as priest and judge? (1 Sam 2:23-25, 27-29; 1 Sam 3:11-14; Lev 5:20-26; Lev 18:20; Lev 20:10; Lev 16)

3. Summarize the differences in the Old Testament priesthood of Eli's time and the New Testament priesthood of today. (CCC 1539-1540, 1544-1545; Heb 9:11-14; CCC 613)

4. How was God working for the benefit of Israel through the troubled time of Eli and his sons? (1 Sam 2:26; 3:1-10, 19-21)

QUESTIONS FOR APPLICATION

1. Have you ever pointed out the sinful behavior of someone close to you? How challenging was that for you? What approach did you take to make the conversation loving and productive?

2. What effects on the Church have you seen from the clerical sex abuse crisis? What have you seen that reassures you that God has not abandoned the Church?

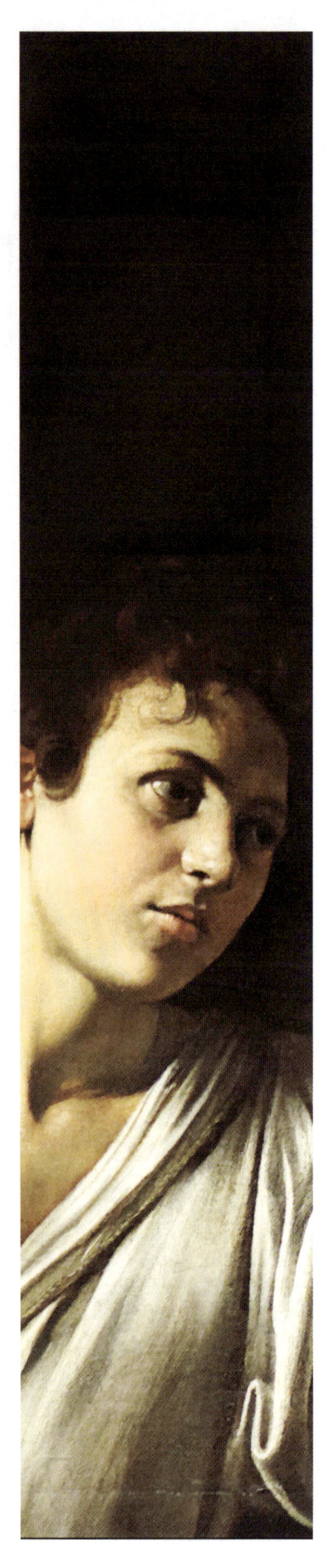

3. Can you think of a great priest in your life whose faithfulness to his vocation has affected you in some way? Please describe.

4. What would be some good ways of supporting the priests you know to help them live out their vocations faithfully and fruitfully?

DAVID THE KING

LESSON THREE
WARRIOR OF GOD

LESSON THREE IMAGE
David with the Head of Goliath. Caravaggio, 1607.
Vienna, Kunsthistorisches Museum.

WARRIOR OF GOD
LESSON THREE OUTLINE

I.   SAUL'S FAILURE AS KING
- A. Did not kill all the Amalekites
- B. God's warriors need to battle evil "all the way down"
- C. Jesus battled evil all the way on the cross

II.   ANNOINTING A NEW KING
- A. Samuel the prophet comes to Bethlehem to annoint a new king
- B. Jesse presents seven oldest sons and all are rejected
- C. David, the youngest, called in from the fields and is annointed
    1. "Spirit of God rushes upon him"
    2. Grace comes first; God chooses us; we respond or not
- D. David summoned to Saul's court
    1. To ease Saul's afflictions with his music ("sweet singer of Israel")
    2. Sent to Philistine battlefield to bring provisions
- E. David faces Goliath
    1. Goliath imposing and covered in heavy armor
    2. David naked and clothed with the love, mercy, and non-violence of God just as Jesus was on the cross

DAVID THE KING

LESSON THREE
WARRIOR OF GOD

In the third talk, Bishop Barron introduces us to Saul, to his fall from grace, to David, and to David's anointing as Saul's replacement. For the purpose of putting David's story in context, it would be helpful for us to go through the story of Saul first so that we can better understand the story of David, which Bishop Barron unpacks for us.

†

SAUL

Samuel Replaces Eli as Prophet, Priest, and Judge

After the death of Eli, we find out the true extent of Eli's failings through a subtle remark on the part of Samuel:

> Then Samuel addressed the whole house of Israel: "If you would return to the LORD with your whole heart, remove your foreign gods and your Astartes, fix your hearts on the LORD, and serve him alone, then the LORD will deliver you from the hand of the Philistines." (1 Sam 7:3)

Evidently the sacrificial cult of Israel had been so badly abused that many people were driven away from it, just as people today have been driven away from the Church by the sexual abuse crisis. Even back then this was not a new problem. We read in the Book of Judges that this had happened before (Judges 10:6), and so in the first book of Samuel God continues the pattern he had established in the Book of Judges. When the people fall into the worship of foreign gods, he delivers the people into the hands of their enemies. Then he sends someone to deliver them and to restore them to the worship of the Lord.

DAVID THE KING

37

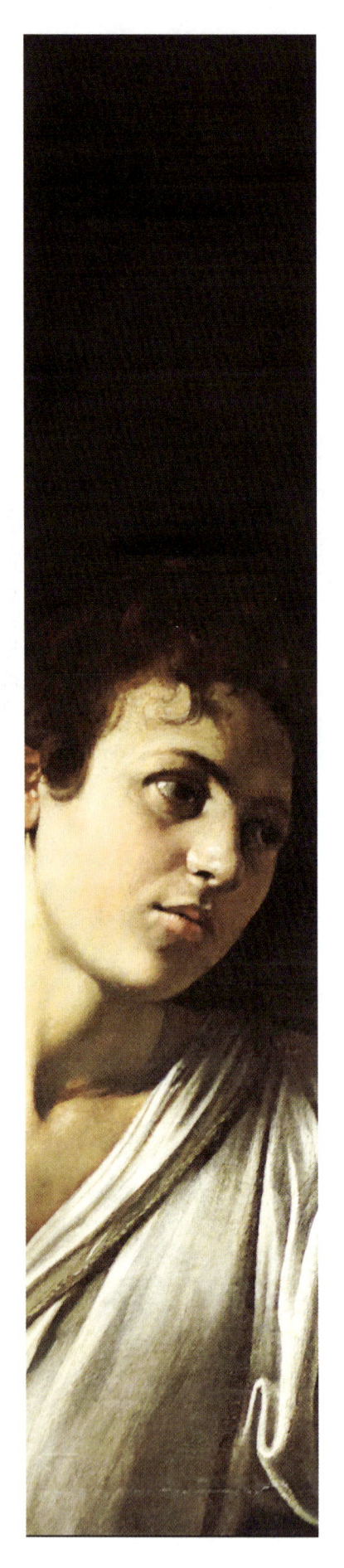

This time the righteous one is Samuel. Eli was supposed to be a priest, a prophet, and a judge, but had lost his faith, lost his sight, and lost his will to execute judgment. Samuel is his replacement. We already know that he is a powerful prophet, which gives us hope for a fruitful priesthood and judicial leadership.

As judge and priest, Samuel is initially successful. One of his first acts is to gather Israel together to battle the Philistines. In order to command them successfully, Samuel exercises his priestly ministry by leading them in fasting and prayer (1 Sam 7:5-8). The culmination of his prayer is a whole burnt offering (1 Sam 7:9). During the burnt offering the Philistines attack. Because the Israelites have turned back to the Lord, they are not only victorious over the Philistines; they rout them (1 Sam 7:10-11).

At the end of Samuel's life the pattern of Eli repeats itself, only this time with respect to the judicial office. That office was supposed to be a one-time appointment by God for a specific time, but Samuel tries to make it like a kingship by appointing his sons as his successors. It is a dramatic failure. "His sons did not walk in his ways, but turned aside after gain; they took bribes and perverted justice" (1 Sam 8:3). Samuel's sons do for the judicial office what Eli's sons did for the priesthood.

Just as Eli's abuse of the priesthood led the people away from the sacrificial cult that God had established, so likewise Samuel's sons' abuse of the judicial office leads the people away from the judicial system that God had established:

> Therefore all the elders of Israel assembled and went to Samuel at Ramah and said to him, "Now that you are old, and your sons do not follow your example, appoint a king over us, like all the nations, to rule us." (1 Sam 8:4-5)

The request is ironic. Samuel had been turning the judicial system into a monarchy. The people ask for king as though it is going to get them out of the problems they think they are having with the judicial system. What they don't realize is that they are asking for the very thing that is causing the problems in the first place!

Israel Requests a King to Replace God

If we want to understand the literal sense of the dialogue that follows among God, Samuel, and the people of Israel, it is important for us to read it primarily with a biblical lens and not an American lens, to contextualize it in terms of the Deuteronomic covenant and not to import assumptions about the nature of kings. The reason for this is that Scripture does not see kingship as inherently evil in the way that many American historians portray it. Biblically, it is not that kings are bad *per se*. Indeed, the Lord himself is a King (Deut 33:5). Kingship is good in itself, but like any good it can be easily perverted if used by someone evil. The question to ask of a given king is whether he is trying to *replace* God or to *serve* God. This is the same question that the Church teaches us to ask about any form of government, whether monarchy, democracy, or anything in between (CCC 2442).

The Israelites later explain why they are requesting a king: "that we also may be like all the nations, and that our king may govern us and go out before us and fight our battles" (1 Sam 8:20). If we consider these words against the background of the judicial system, we can see that they constitute a drastic lack of fidelity to the Deuteronomic covenant. It was the Lord who governed the people and gave them the judicial system; it was the Lord who raised up the judges; it was the Lord who empowered the judges: and it was the Lord who ensured the victory of the judges against their enemies. The Israelites' request for a king is at its heart an act of idolatry. It is a violation of the first commandment of the Law, just like the worship of the Golden Calf.

It is in this light that the Lord responds to the request for a king. Putting Samuel in his place by reminding him that he is a judge and not a king, the Lord says:

> Listen to whatever the people say. You are not the one they are rejecting. They are rejecting me as their king. They are acting toward you just as they have acted from the day I brought them up from Egypt to this very day, deserting me to serve other gods. Now listen to them; but at the same time, give them a solemn warning and inform them of the rights of the king who will rule them.
> (1 Sam 8:7-9)

Samuel goes on to describe the nature of *the specific king* who is going to reign over the Israelites as a result of their making an idolatrous request (1 Sam 8:10-18). Samuel is not giving a general description of the nature of kings as such. Remember, a monarchy—like a democracy—can be good or evil based on how it serves or does not serve the Lord. Israel asks for a king to replace God rather than to serve God. God says to Israel, "Thy will be done." The Israelites' punishment is going to consist in the granting of their request. It is going to be—quite literally—hellish to live under a king who does not serve God (see Cyprian, Ep. 64.1).

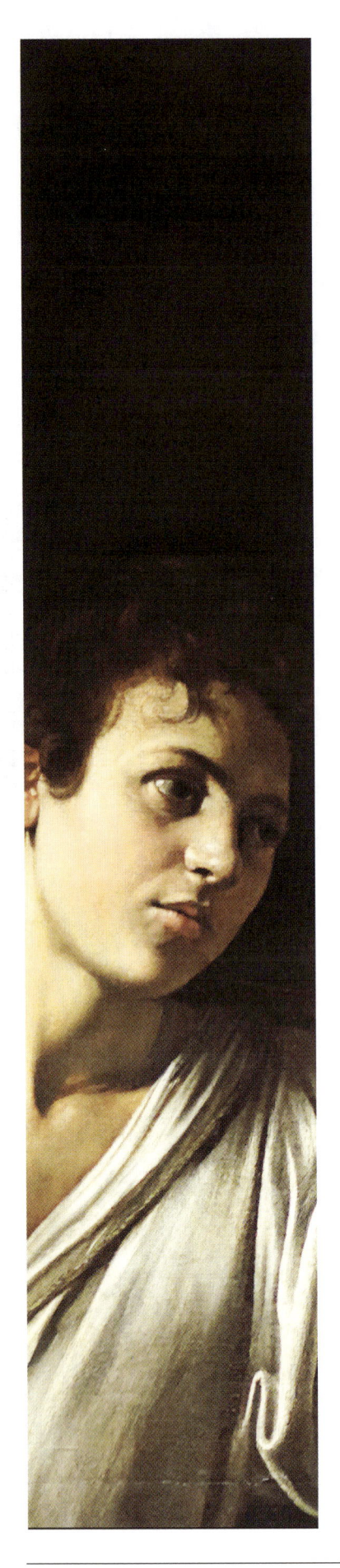

Thereupon Samuel gives them the famous description of this king:

> He told them: "The governance of the king who will rule you will be as follows: He will take your sons and assign them to his chariots and horses, and they will run before his chariot. He will appoint from among them his commanders of thousands and of hundreds. He will make them do his plowing and harvesting and produce his weapons of war and chariotry. He will use your daughters as perfumers, cooks, and bakers. He will take your best fields, vineyards, and olive groves, and give them to his servants. He will tithe your crops and grape harvests to give to his officials and his servants.
>
> He will take your male and female slaves, as well as your best oxen and donkeys, and use them to do his work. He will also tithe your flocks. As for you, you will become his slaves. On that day you will cry out because of the king *whom you have chosen*, but the LORD will not answer you on that day."
> (1 Sam 8:11-18; emphasis added)

Saul becomes King

God's choice of Saul does not initially seem in line with Samuel's solemn admonition. In fact, it seems like Saul is well positioned to teach the Israelites the same lesson they will later learn from David's defeat of Goliath. Saul, we are told, is from the humblest family of the humblest tribe of Israel (1 Sam 9:21). By profession he is a donkey herdsman. To add to Saul's humility, all the donkeys are lost and he has to wander through several lands in order to find them (1 Sam 9:3). If the Lord is going to choose him as king then it would seem that the Lord is setting up to show forth great things through such a humble person. However, as Bishop Barron will note also about David, Saul has a weakness: he is good-looking. "There was not a man among the sons of Israel more handsome than he; from his shoulders upward he was taller than any of the people." (1 Sam 9:2) This is the first clue we are given that there are going to be problems with Saul. The second clue is hidden in his profession. Saul herds an animal that is just as stubborn as he is!

Saul's ascent to power is almost instantaneous. While he is looking around for the donkeys, his servant suggests that they look for the prophet who is in town (1 Sam 9:5-10). It turns out to be Samuel (1 Sam 9:15-26). Samuel, having tried to turn the judicial office into a kingship, is now charged with anointing the king who will abolish the judicial office (1 Sam 9:15-16). All throughout their visit Samuel says nothing to Saul about the fact that the Lord has appointed Saul king. But finally, just as Saul is about to go on his way, even as Samuel is saying goodbye, it happens—almost as an afterthought:

> Then, from a flask he had with him, Samuel poured oil on Saul's head and kissed him, saying: "The LORD anoints you ruler over his people Israel. You are the one who will govern the LORD's people and save them from the power of their enemies all around them." (1 Sam 10:1)

In these few words, Samuel describes how good kingship is essentially analogous to the judicial office by which Israel was formerly led. The king does not own the people; he holds the people in trust for the Lord. Also note second the task of the king. Having subordinated himself to the Lord as a servant of the Lord's people, he will save the people from their enemies just as the judges did. Indeed, Samuel later says that the people have the same opportunity for faithfulness under a king as they did under the judges (1 Sam 12:14-15). And although Samuel may not rule the people as judge any more, they can still count on him as a faithful priest and prophet.

Of course, if any person, even a prophet of God, anointed you as a king seemingly out of nowhere, you might be a bit skeptical. As we saw in Lesson 2, even high-level servants of God, like priests, could choose the wrong side of God's political arrangements. So the Lord, working through Samuel, gives Saul an elaborate confirmation of the reality of his kingship through prophecy. Samuel prophecies in detail all the events that are going to take place in Saul's life in the near future, culminating in a trip to Gilgal, where Saul is to wait seven days until Samuel arrives to offer a burnt offering (1 Sam 10:2-8). This is to be a sort of test for Saul. If he remains faithful to the Lord, arrives at Gilgal, and waits the seven days for Samuel to offer the burnt offering, he passes the test and the Lord will establish his kingdom forever (1 Sam 13:13). If not, consequences will follow.

Initially, things go well and events come to pass as God said they would. In the midst of it all Saul musters 330,000 people and leads them out to battle against the Ammonites. It's enough to replace the 30,000 slain under Eli's disastrous defeat, plus ten times more (1 Sam 11:8). As the Philistines were routed under Samuel as judge, so the Ammonites are scattered under Saul as king (1 Sam 11:11). The success makes it seem as though Saul were a faithful replacement for Samuel.

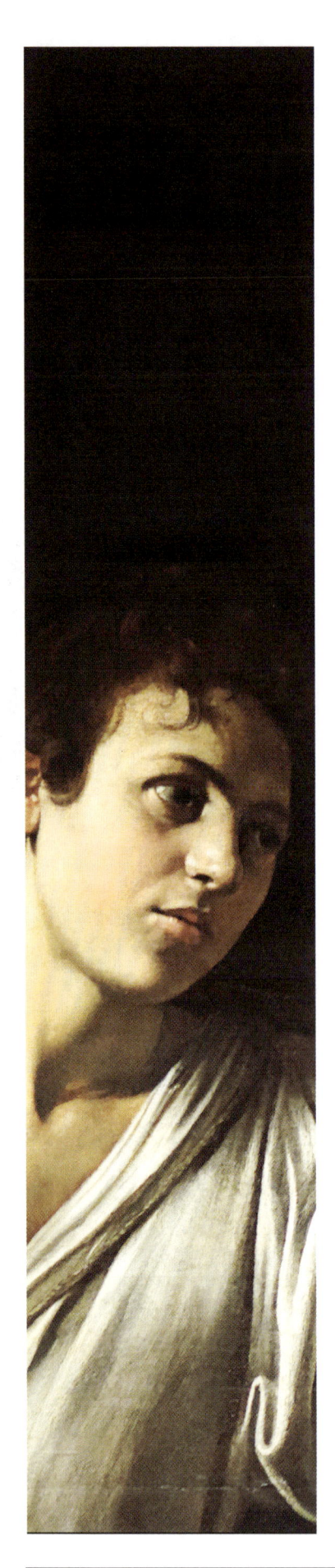

Saul does not ultimately pass the test, however, and so his fall is almost as rapid as his ascent. After his quick defeat of the Ammonites, Saul—perhaps feeling self-satisfied—sends most of his men home; he only keeps 3,000 behind with him: 2,000 for himself, and 1,000 for his son, Jonathan (1 Sam 13:2). What is more, Jonathan manages to defeat a garrison of the Philistines with his 1,000 men, a victory which the people attribute to Saul (1 Sam 13:3-4). This enrages the Philistines, and they come out in force against Saul with "thirty thousand chariots, and six thousand horsemen, and troops like the sand on the seashore in multitude" (1 Sam 13:5). Saul is outgunned and outnumbered. He is outgunned, because the chariots and the weapons of the Philistines are made of iron, a metal which the Israelites lack. He is outnumbered, because from among the few men he has left, people start deserting out of fear. Saul winds up with what later turns out to be only 600 men (1 Sam 13:15).

Fearing for his life, and despairing of Samuel's aid, Saul does the unthinkable: he usurps Samuel's office and offers the burnt offering himself (1 Sam 13:9). Samuel appears, and Saul tries to pass it off as Samuel's failure (1 Sam 13:11-12). But Samuel is not so easily fooled. He knows that Saul is just trying to cover up for his own failure. Samuel decrees the sentence of the Lord: "But now your kingdom shall not continue; the Lord has sought out a man after his own heart; and the Lord has appointed him to be prince over his people, because you have not kept what the Lord commanded you" (1 Sam 13:14) This is the first indication that Saul will be replaced as king over Israel because he sought to replace God.

The second indication that Saul will be replaced is given to us in response to a second military and spiritual failure. Thanks to a surprise attack from Saul's son, Jonathan, the Philistine army is put to confusion (1 Sam 14), and the Israelites fight them to a standstill; each nation decides to retire and go back to its own land (1 Sam 14:46). Now that he has rest from the Philistines, the Lord commands him through Samuel to go and put the ban on the Amalekites. As Bishop Barron describes, the ban involved the complete destruction of whatever was under it. This means that the Israelites were commanded to destroy all the people and all the spoils of war, to take nothing for themselves (1 Sam 15:3).

Just as Saul did not completely obey the Lord regarding the seven day test, so neither does he obey the Lord regarding the ban on the Amalekites. The reason he disobeys the Lord is that he fears the people (1 Sam 15:24). The people had previously opposed him once before—Saul had commanded no one to eat until he had been avenged, but Jonathan led the people in taking food (1 Sam 14:24-45). Saul was now afraid that if he did not give the people a high profile prisoner and the best of the spoils, they would oppose him again. So instead of putting all of the Amalekites to the ban, Saul spared their king and let the Israelites keep all the best livestock for themselves (1 Sam 15:8-9).

When Samuel comes out to meet Saul, Saul acts as though nothing is wrong: "Blessed be you to the Lord; I have performed the commandment of the Lord" (1 Sam 15:13). But Samuel calls him out and asks why, if Saul has been so faithful, Samuel can hear sheep bleating and oxen lowing (1 Sam 15:14)? It takes several rounds of interrogation before we come to the point of it. Samuel tells Saul that the Lord has taken the kingship away from him: "You have rejected the word of the Lord, and the Lord has rejected you from being king over Israel" (1 Sam 15:26). Samuel does not at this point say exactly when it will take effect. All the same, Saul gets so angry that he lays hold of Samuel and tears his robe (1 Sam 15:27). That is the last straw. Samuel admonishes him: "The Lord has torn the kingdom of Israel from you this day, and has given it to a neighbor of yours, who is better than you" (1 Sam 15:27).

Saul does finally come to his senses and repent (1 Sam 15:30), but not until it is too late to get the kingdom back (1 Sam 15:29). Thereafter Samuel is directed by God to go and find Saul's successor. That brings us to David.

†

DAVID

David is supposed to restore the era of peace that has been lost under Saul by being a king to serve the Lord rather than a king to replace the Lord. He is a "man after [God's] own heart" (1 Sam 13:14; CCC 2579). Even his name foreshadows what he will be. "David" comes from the Hebrew word "Dōd," meaning "beloved." David is to be the king beloved of God, while Saul was a failed king.

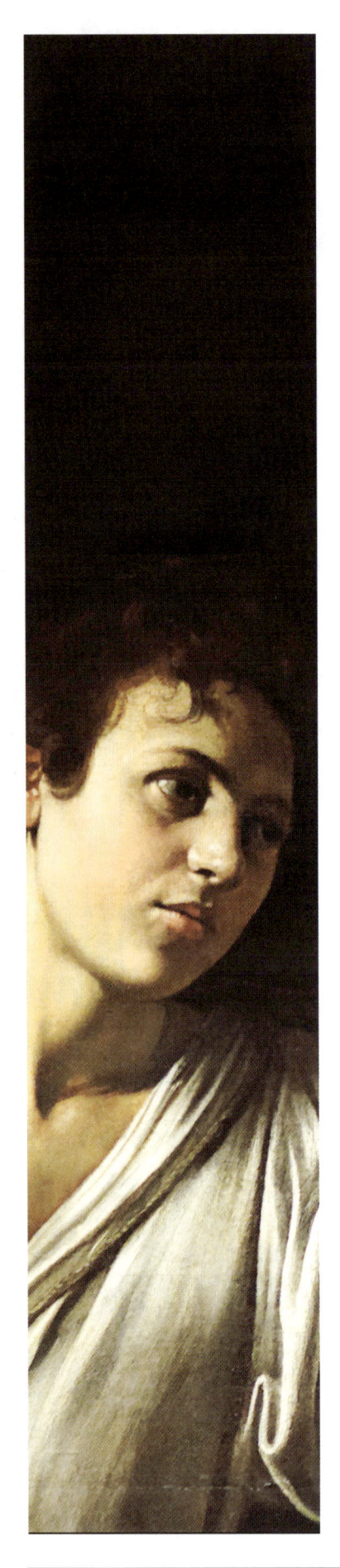

David Is Anointed King

Returning to an era of peace, as Bishop Barron indicates, meant returning to Bethlehem, to the place where our Marian figure, Ruth, made her home and where God restored her to fruitfulness. So it was to that city that God sent Samuel to find David, who will be a figure of Christ. During the meal after the peace offering Samuel has a good opportunity to survey the sons of Jesse and to see which one the Lord has chosen to replace Saul. But Samuel has trouble finding the right candidate. As Bishop Barron explains, that is because David is even humbler than Saul was at the outset. While Saul stood head and shoulders *above* his fellow men, David stands head and shoulders *below* them. He is, in fact, a small shepherd boy, someone whom no one would mistake for king, neither Samuel nor Jesse. He is so insignificant in his family that they do not invite him to the sacrifice. He has to stay home tending the sheep while they worship and socialize with Samuel (1 Sam 16:11). As Bishop Barron points out there is one thing about David that will get him into trouble. He may not be tall, but he is good-looking (1 Sam 16:12). That won't trouble us now, but it will cost David dearly later in the incident with Bathsheba.

The anointing of David as king is almost as abrupt as the anointing of Saul. "And the Lord said, 'Arise, anoint him; for this is he.' Then Samuel took the horn of oil, and anointed him in the midst of his brothers; and the Spirit of the Lord came mightily upon David from that day forward" (1 Sam 16:12-13). However, there is a significant difference between this and Saul's anointing. Hampered by his pride and stubbornness (remember the donkeys?), Saul did not receive the Spirit of the Lord as soon as he was anointed. He had to wait until he was ready for it (1 Sam 10:10). With David it is otherwise. If Saul's livestock symbolize his stubbornness, David's symbolize his meekness—sheep are the animals that Jesus will later use as a symbol of the just because they so readily attend to the voice of their shepherd (Matt 25:32-33). On account of David's meekness, there is no barrier to David's immediate reception of the Spirit. Thus from the moment of his royal anointing, David is filled with the Spirit. This shows us the theological principle that Bishop Barron describes, *gratia prima* (grace first). Saul is a failure because his kingship begins under his own effort; David will be a success because his kingship begins with the grace of God, and because David's kingship continues in cooperation with that grace.

The contrast between David and Saul continues. Evidently with the Spirit of the Lord rushing upon David, the Spirit of the Lord rushed *out* of Saul; and when the Spirit of the Lord departs, there is room for the demons of this world to move in (1 Sam 16:14). Saul looks around to find someone to lift his spirits, and he hears of David. In spite of the fact that David is still only a boy and still tending sheep (1 Sam 16:19), he has acquired quite a reputation: "skillful in playing, a man of valor, a man of war, prudent in speech, and a man of good presence; and the Lord is with him" (1 Sam 16:18). Note the contrast. We are told that when Samuel first came to David: "the Lord sees not as man sees; man looks on the outward appearance, but the Lord looks on the heart" (1 Sam 16:7). The first part of David's reputation speaks to his outward appearance; only the last line, "the Lord is with him," speaks to his inward character. Saul is under the impression that David's outward qualities, particularly his musical skill, are what will make him feel better. But the irony that Saul does not know is that David brings with him the Spirit of the Lord that Saul has lost.

The complete contrast between Saul and David is sealed by a small event that happens next. David is beloved not just by God but by Saul as well, so Saul appoints him to be his armor-bearer. Thereafter he sends a message to David's father, Jesse, asking for David to remain in his service (1 Sam 16:21-22). With that we have the first indication that Samuel's prophecy of an evil king has come to pass in Saul. Saul has "taken" Jesse's son, just as Samuel had predicted an evil king would do.

David and Goliath

In the next scene, the fulfillment of Samuel's prophecy about an evil king continues. The Philistines have come out to battle against the Israelites. The two armies are encamped upon opposing mountains (1 Sam 17:3). This is the ancient version of trench warfare. In World War I, trench warfare was the way in which opposing armies attempted to avoid one another's gunfire. By digging into a trench, soldiers were safe from the shots fired overhead. The difficulty was that once a company of soldiers was in a trench, it was very difficult to get them out; the first side to leave the trench could be easily gunned down. In ancient Israel, camping on opposing mountains was similar because it put the two sides at a distance from which neither could hurt the other. But their safety was also their liability. Neither side could afford to rush down first, because it would give the other side a tactical height advantage, and make them easy prey for their opponents. Into this fruitless stalemate Saul has conscripted thousands of Israelite men (see 1 Sam 17:13-18), just as Samuel had predicted.

In order to break the stalemate, a Philistine named Goliath comes down and proposes that the contest be decided by man-to-man combat (1 Sam 17:9). He is a fearsome opponent.

Bishop Barron draws our attention to the careful and frightful description that the Deuteronomistic Historian paints of him:

- Goliath is 9 ft. 9 in. tall.
- He has a coat of mail weighing anywhere from 121 lbs. to 187 lbs. By comparison, a full suit of medieval plate mail weighed only about 50 lbs.
- He has a spear whose head alone weighs anywhere from 14.5 lbs. to 22.5 lbs. By comparison, an Olympic men's shot-put weighs 16 lbs.
- He is also wearing a helmet, shin-guards, and other armor besides the coat of mail (1 Sam 17:5-7).

David, by contrast, is no warrior at all. His father has sent him on an errand to bring provisions to his older brothers (1 Sam 17:17-18), and when he tarries too long one of his older brothers chides him for neglecting the sheep (1 Sam 17:28-30). Yet when David hears of the Philistine's challenge, his zeal for God is kindled and he volunteers to fight (1 Sam 17:32).

David's preparations for battle reflect his humble background. At first the Israelites figure that the best way to prepare David to oppose the Philistine is to make his outward appearance similar, so they give him a helmet, a coat of mail, and a sword (1 Sam 17:38-39). But the battle array is so heavy that David cannot move in it (1 Sam 17:39). So David instead assumes the trappings of his profession: he puts aside the armor and the sword, grabs his slingshot, and picks up five stones—one for each book of the Law.

The battle between David and Goliath is a dramatization of the principle announced earlier: man looks on the outside, but the Lord looks in the heart. On the outside, David and Israel appear doomed. David's only hope appears to be in his five stones. If he misses with those, if he hits Goliath but Goliath is not stopped, or if Goliath gets to him before he has had a chance to land an incapacitating blow, David seems assured of death. But on the inside, David's hope is in the Lord, and in the Law of the Lord, represented by those five stones. As he approaches the battle, he picks up his staff and so appears as a figure of Moses, by whom God delivered the Israelites out of the hand of the Egyptians (1 Sam 17:40). From God's perspective Goliath is as doomed to failure as David appears to be from ours; and David slays Goliath with one stone from the slingshot (1 Sam 17:49). With Goliath dead, the Philistines flee and Israel despoils them.

Thanks to David's faithfulness, victory returns to Israel once more (1 Sam 17:52-54). David has not yet had an opportunity to completely assume his authority as Saul's replacement, but he nevertheless gives us the biblical picture of a good king. The good king, like the good judge, serves the Lord and does not seek to replace him. Just as God promised, God delivers Israel by the hand of the good king from its enemies and gives them rest.

The Allegorical and Anagogical Senses

As Bishop Barron interprets the stories of Saul and David for us, we see in David an allegorical figure of Jesus. There are a number of signs pointing us to that identification. At the outset we see that David is the eighth son of Jesse. The number eight, as Bishop Barron indicates, evokes an "eternal dimension." It is a figure of the eternal Sabbath rest after the eight day, of the never-ending Resurrection which follows the week of the Passion.

The second thing that points us to see Christ in David is that he is a "christ." As Bishop Barron explains, the English word "Christ" is a transliteration of the Greek word *christos*, which is a translation of the Hebrew word *Mashiach*—Messiah, "anointed one." David is an anointed man of God who comes to deliver people from bondage to an evil king and to give them the opportunity to serve the Lord through the reign of a good king.

The third thing that points us to see Christ in David is the manner in which he does battle. Bishop Barron connects the story of David with Michelangelo's statue of David, in which David is portrayed as was Christ on the cross: naked. We have here an indication of a return to Eden. Prior to the Fall, Adam and Eve "were naked and were not ashamed" (Gen 2:25). Owing to his complete fidelity to the Lord, David is unafraid to do battle naked, even against a giant Philistine in super-armor. David's nakedness represents the nakedness of Christ, who conquers sin and the hosts of Satan with the power of the Cross.

The three aforementioned similarities between Christ and David are all exterior. Let us recall, however, the principle from 1 Samuel that "man looks on the outward appearance, but the Lord looks on the heart." While we may look to David's exterior nakedness and see an affinity with Jesus, the Lord was more concerned about David's interior nakedness, about his lack of guile, about the meekness he had in the presence of grace. David's single greatest Christological quality is his radical fidelity to the Lord.

DAVID THE KING

47

David's fidelity, seen allegorically in the light of Christ, leads us to the anagogical reading of this story that Bishop Barron proposes for us to consider. According to this sense of the story, Saul and David represent our souls as we struggle to do battle with the darkness of evil in our own lives. God's call, which he has addressed to his people over the centuries, and which he addresses to each one of us today, is a call to radical holiness. "Be holy, as I am holy." (See Lev 11:44-45; 1 Pet 1:16; *Lumen gentium*, 40). Radical holiness means, as Bishop Barron teaches us, "not making any compromises with evil."

Evil in our lives is symbolized by the nations that war against Israel. Their armaments symbolize the defenses we put up against the grace of God that would heal us. God's charge to Saul to put the Amalekites to the ban represents God's charge to each of us to destroy whatever comes between us and himself. Saul's failure to be faithful represents what happens when we only follow the Lord halfway. Saul's loss of the kingship represents the drastic consequences that can happen to us if we make too many compromises with evil—we may tragically lose everything we hold dear.

But David gives us hope. David represents how it is possible to be radically faithful to the Lord, to make no compromises with evil, to be meek before grace, to put down all our barriers to the Lord, and to be transformed in his love. When that happens, the Goliaths in our lives don't stand a fighting chance. From all outward appearances it may seem that we have been overcome, trod down, worn thin by the evils and cares of this world. But if we make no compromises, if we cling to the Lord, if we take as our weapons the words of the Lord, then we can overcome even the fiercest of obstacles, particularly those that we ourselves have erected to keep the Lord at a distance from our deepest wounds.

QUESTIONS FOR UNDERSTANDING

1. What was wrong with the Israelites' request for a king? (1 Sam 8:4-9, 19-20; Deut 33:1-5)

2. What were the two sins that got the kingship taken away from Saul? (1 Sam 10:2-8; 13:8-13; 15:1-9)

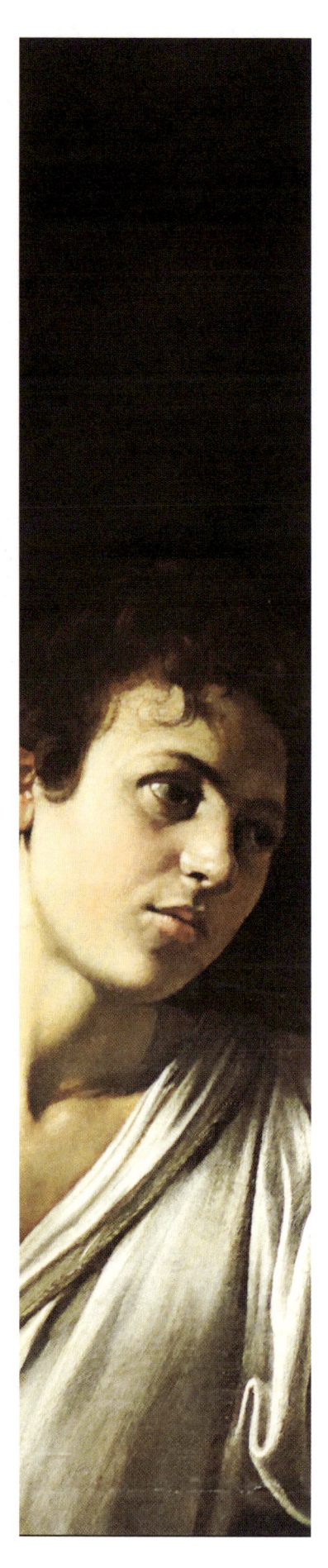

3. How does David's battle with Goliath illustrate the principle *gratia prima* ("grace first"), and how do soldiers of God fight? (1 Sam 16:13; CCC 2008-2010; CCC 2306)

4. How is David a figure of Christ? (Acts 13:22; Ps 119:2-3, 47-48)

QUESTIONS FOR APPLICATION

1. How is your own (local, state, national) government faring with respect to biblical criteria for good government?

2. In what areas of your own life do you experience the temptation to look for a worldly king instead of God?

3. Where does David's refusal to compromise with evil resonate most with the challenges of your daily life?

4. How are you pursuing "radical holiness"?

DAVID THE KING

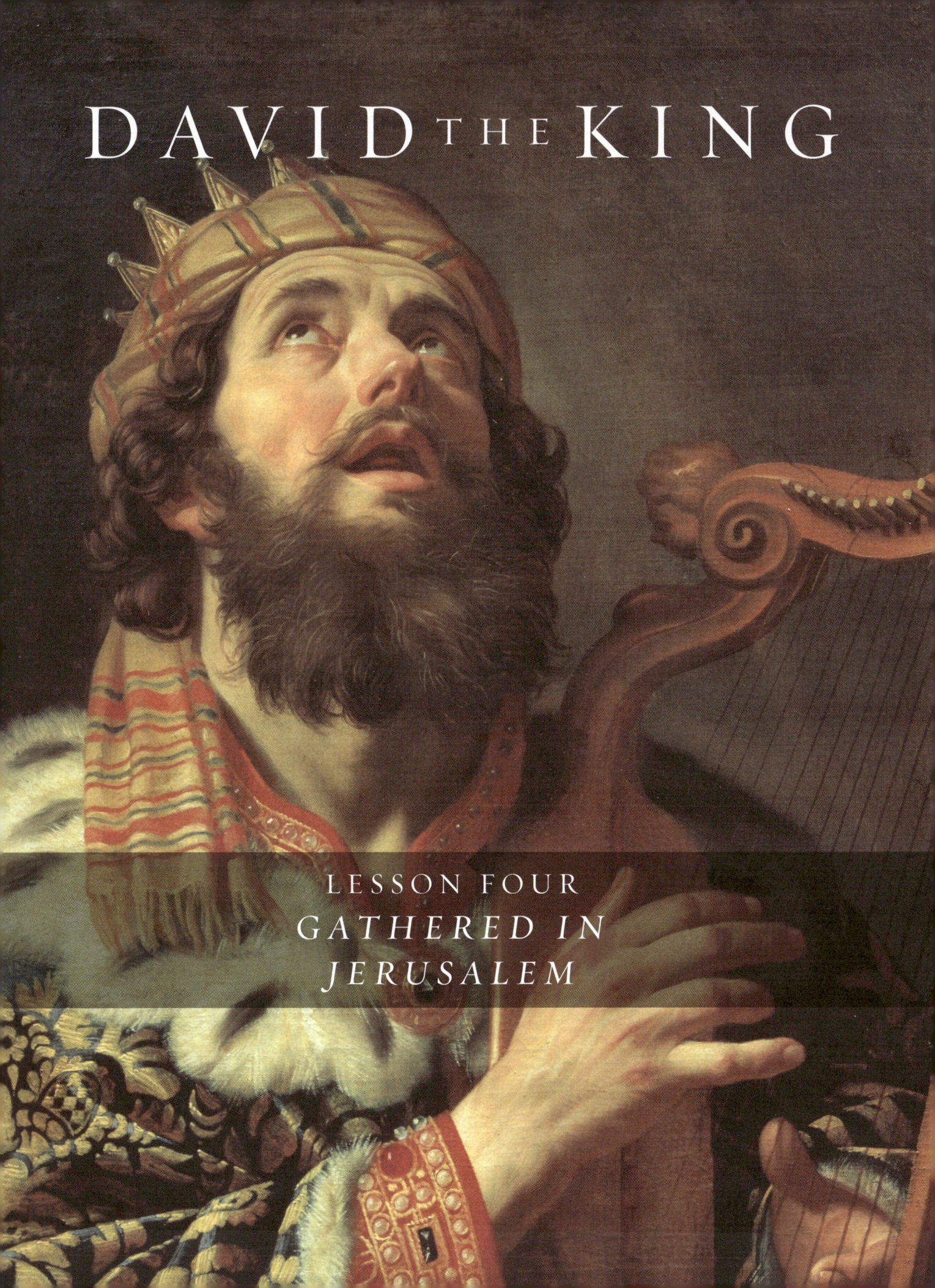

LESSON FOUR
GATHERED IN
JERUSALEM

LESSON FOUR IMAGE
King David Playing the Harp. Gerard van Honthorst, 1622.
Netherlands, Centraal Museum in Utrecht.

GATHERED IN JERUSALEM
LESSON FOUR OUTLINE

I. SAUL AGAINST DAVID
    A. Israel is divided against itself due to conflict between Saul and David
    B. Demonic influence: *diabolos* (Greek) meaning the "one who divides"
    C. David flees from Saul, but does not attack him even with several opportunities
    D. When Saul and his son Jonathan die, David sings a beautiful elegy, further exhibiting his Christlike attitude of nonviolence.

II. DAVID UNITES THE TRIBES OF ISRAEL IN JERUSALEM
    A. Body of Israel forming after years of exile: foreshadows the mystical body of Christ
    B. David conquers Jerusalem and makes it Israel's capital and center
    C. David gathers all of Israel, as all nations will be gathered in Christ in the future

III. JERUSALEM BECOMES THE CENTER OF "RIGHT PRAISE"
    A. David moves the Ark of the Covenant from Shiloh to Jerusalem in procession
    B. Man struck down by God while trying to steady the Ark on the ox cart
    C. Difficult for us humans to understand why God struck him down
        1. God has a prescribed way to move the ark, which David violated
        2. God always appears to us to be a little strange and inscrutable because he cannot be categorized
    D. David dances before the Ark and before the Law as it comes into Jerusalem
        1. Symbolizes Israel finding its proper rhythm again, united and centered on God
        2. Connection between the Ark and Mary, who carries within her the very Word of God

DAVID THE KING

LESSON FOUR
GATHERED IN JERUSALEM

In the fourth talk, Bishop Barron moves on from the story of David and Goliath and takes us through four pivotal aspects of David's ascendency to the royal throne: the struggle with Saul, the union of the tribes, the priesthood of David, and the liturgical procession into Jerusalem.

THE STRUGGLE BETWEEN SAUL AND DAVID

In the literal sense, the next thing that happens in the story of David is his struggle with Saul. "Why," you might ask, "would there be a struggle between Saul and David if Saul knew that the Lord had taken away his kingdom and David knew that the Lord had given it to himself?" The answer is that, although Samuel had informed Saul that the Lord had taken the kingdom away, he did not tell Saul exactly to whom he was going to give it, nor did Saul know that Samuel had by this point already anointed David.

Saul does at least see that David is growing in influence among the subjects of the kingdom (1 Sam 18:9); though, unbeknownst to him, this also includes Saul's own son and heir, Jonathan (1 Sam 18:1-5). Still, considering only how things appear on the outside, Saul thinks that he can stop David's rise by killing him. He secretly hurls a spear at David while David is playing the lyre within Saul's house (1 Sam 18:10-11). However, "David evaded him twice" (1 Sam 18:11).

What Saul does not realize is that by trying to kill David he will create the very rivalry he is hoping to quell by murdering him. To return to a theme that Bishop Barron highlighted in the first talk, God, in his Providence, often turns the momentum of evil against itself—like in the martial art aikido. Saul's jealousy over David's popularity and his attempts to take David's life begin a spiral of events that solidify David's hold over the kingdom and gradually reveal to Saul the truth of David's accession to the throne.

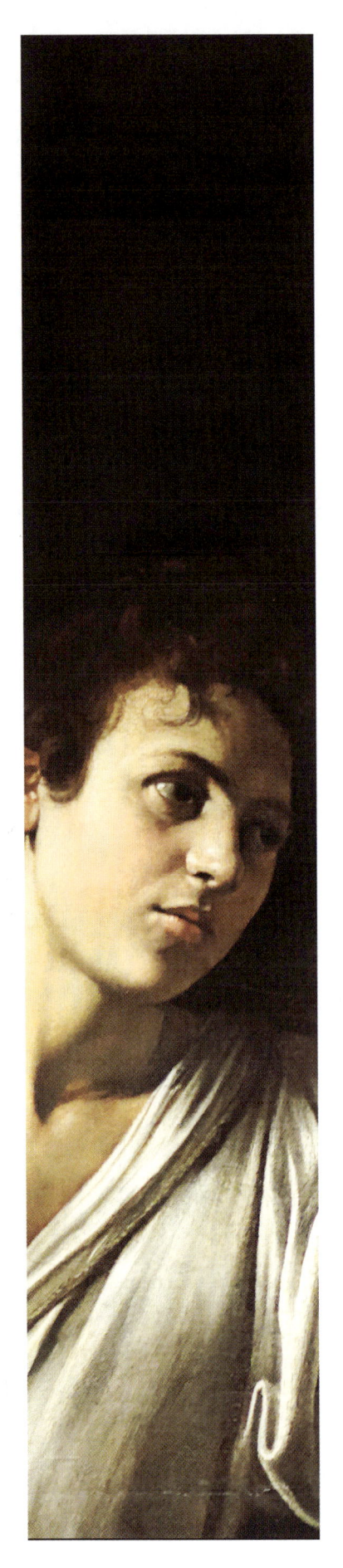

Over time, Saul begins to figure things out (1 Sam 18:12). But he still wants to kill David secretly, so he devises a plan to entrap David: he will offer David his daughter Michal in marriage, provided that David goes out and kills a hundred Philistines (1 Sam 18:20-26). Of course, we can see how blinded Saul is by his jealousy to come up with such a bad idea—David has a history with Philistines! So we are not surprised when the result is a disaster from Saul's perspective. David kills *two* hundred Philistines, and Saul is forced to give his daughter away in marriage to him (1 Sam 18:26-27). Now, by God's providential aikido, David has the allegiance both of Saul's son and his daughter.

From that point forward, David—aided by Jonathan and Michal—travels around the kingdom in an effort to escape Saul's murderous envy, and people rally to him from every side. First there is Samuel; when Saul and his messengers draw near him, they are incapacitated with the spirit of prophecy (1 Sam 19:18-24). Then there is Ahimelech the priest, a descendent of Eli, who feeds David holy bread and arms him with the sword of Goliath, a sword which David himself is now powerful enough to wield (1 Sam 21:2-10). Before you know it, "every one who was in distress, and every one who was in debt, and every one who was discontented, gathered to him; and he became captain over them. And there were with him about four hundred men" (1 Sam 22:2).

The angrier Saul gets, the more the divine aikido turns his envy against him, and the more people flock to David. At the height of it, Saul gets so angry at the fact that Ahimelech assisted David that he orders the slaughter of Ahimelech and all of the priests with him (1 Sam 22:17). But Saul's guard, presumably disgusted by the order, refuses to carry it out. Only one person can be found willing to act on that sacrilegious order, and slaughters an entire city of priests: men, women, and children (1 Sam 22:17-19). Yet just as Saul had earlier refused the Lord's command to put the Amalekites under the ban, so also the Lord refuses Saul's wish to put the priests under the ban; the Lord allows Ahimelech's son, Abiathar, to escape. Thanks to Saul's rampage, Abiathar is practically driven into the service of David (1 Sam 23:6), and, like his father before him, Abiathar arms David. But where Ahimelech had armed David with a temporal weapon, Abiathar arms him with a spiritual one. He brings David the ephod of the priest. Although David does not wear it until he takes possession of Jerusalem, he uses it as a sacramental to take counsel with the Lord (1 Sam 23:6, 9).

©2017 Word on Fire Catholic Ministries

Now the tables are turned completely. Thanks to God turning the momentum of Saul's envy against itself, David has the Spirit of the Lord as well as the allegiance of Saul's heir, Saul's daughter, Saul's priests, Saul's guard, and Saul's peasants. Then David does something that finally shocks Saul out of his blinding envy into the light the truth. He sneaks up on Saul while Saul is relieving himself and cuts off the skirt of Saul's robe (1 Sam 24:4). When David reveals the fact to Saul, as well as the fact that he had the opportunity to kill Saul but chose not to, Saul realizes that he has been bested (1 Sam 24:17-22).

With Saul's realization that David is to be king over Israel, the beginning of the end—even if not the absolute end—of the conflict between David and Saul has arrived. Thus the ministry for which the Lord had commissioned Samuel is complete, and we are told in one quick verse that "Samuel died; and all Israel assembled and mourned for him, and they buried him in his house at Ramah" (1 Sam 25:1). Just as John the Baptist, the last forerunner to the Lord, would later declare, "he must increase, but I must decrease" (John 3:30), so the earlier men of God each give way to the later ones. With David assured of victory over Saul, Samuel passes into the reward for which he had long labored, and David rises as yet a clearer figure of Christ.

✝

THE DEATH OF SAUL

Toward the end of his life, Saul is easily persuaded to pursue David again (1 Sam 26:1). Things turn out no differently the second time around. As before, David evades Saul, and then spares Saul when given the chance to kill him (1 Sam 26:6-12). Also as before, Saul speaks words that seem apologetic:

> Then Saul said, "I have done wrong; return, my son David, for I will no more do you harm, because my life was precious in your eyes this day; behold, I have played the fool, and have erred exceedingly." (1 Sam 26:21)

Outwardly it would seem as though Saul were truly repentant. But David, looking more towards Saul's heart than towards his words, still reserves judgment:

> And David said in his heart, "I shall now perish one day by the hand of Saul; there is nothing better for me than that I should escape to the land of the Philistines; then Saul will despair of seeking me any longer within the borders of Israel, and I shall escape out of his hand." (1 Sam 27:1)

DAVID THE KING

After David has lived among them for a while, the Philistines decide to fight against the Israelites. It is a disastrous turn of events for Saul. As we saw in Lesson 2, the king inherited what used to be the judge's role of winning battles with the strength of the Lord. Since, therefore, David is the rightful king, Saul cannot be victorious without David.

Implicitly, Saul knows this and despairs. In his sorrow, he gives into the temptation of witchcraft and finds a medium who practices necromancy (1 Sam 28:6-7). He asks her to conjure up Samuel from the dead in the hopes that Samuel will tell him something different from what he already knows (1 Sam 28:11). He should have known better. Samuel obliges the necromancer's inquiry with his usual bluntness and brings the story of Saul full circle:

> Why then do you ask me [about the Philistines], since the Lord has turned from you and become your enemy? The Lord has done to you as he spoke by me; for the Lord has torn the kingdom out of your hand, and given it to your neighbor, David. Because you did not obey the voice of the Lord, and did not carry out his fierce wrath against Amalek, therefore the Lord has done this thing to you this day. Moreover the Lord will give Israel also with you into the hand of the Philistines; and tomorrow you and your sons shall be with me; the Lord will give the army of Israel also into the hand of the Philistines. (1 Sam 28:16-19)

Samuel's reference to the Amalekites is more than a mere reminder of past misdeeds. In the dramatic irony of the divine aikido, without David Saul is going to lose the fight against the Philistines precisely because David will be off finishing Saul's old business with the Amalekites.

David, as usual, is successful (1 Sam 30:17-20). Saul, as usual, is not. The Israelites are routed (1 Sam 31:1); Saul's sons are killed (1 Sam 31:2); then, just as the Philistines are closing in, Saul gives up. He commands his armor-bearer to run him through. But just as Saul's guard turned away from the sacrilegious order to slay the priests, so Saul's armor-bearer turns away from a similar order now (1 Sam 31:4). So Saul takes his own life, and the Philistines take several Israelite cities (1 Sam 31:5-7).

After David finishes his battle against the Amalekites, a messenger arrives (2 Sam 1:1). The messenger figures that if he lies to David and says that he himself killed Saul, David will congratulate him and enrich him (2 Sam 4:10). David does not know that the man is lying, because this is the first news that he has heard from the battle. But that is no matter—even if David had known the man was lying, his concern was for something much more important. This man had gloated about killing someone who had been anointed by God:

> And David said to the young man who told him, "Where do you come from?" And he answered, "I am the son of a sojourner, an Amalekite." David said to him, "How is it you were not afraid to put forth your hand to destroy the Lord's anointed?" Then David called one of the young men and said, "Go, fall upon him." And he struck him so that he died. And David said to him, "Your blood be upon your head; for your own mouth has testified against you, saying, 'I have slain the Lord's anointed.'" (2 Sam 1:13-16)

David's respect for Saul as the Lord's anointed has a solid basis in the Law, and it is part of what makes David a man "after [God's] own heart." The Law included a special anointing oil, radiant with fragrance, "blended as by the perfumer" (Exod 30:25), and set apart from all other oils (Exod 30:33). The purpose of the oil was to set apart people and things for the service of God (Exod 30:26-30). Once something was anointed, its consecration to God was permanent and could not be undone (Exod 30:29). So powerful was the consecrating power of that oil that anyone who used it on what was profane or even made an oil that smelled like it was to be punished with permanent exile (Exod 30:33).

Initially, the anointing oil was reserved for the consecration of priests. However, in due course it also came to be used on those set apart for two other sacred offices: prophets and kings. It represented a pouring out of the Holy Spirit, which is why Jesus is said to have been "anointed with the Holy Spirit" (Acts 10:38; CCC 695).

There is, therefore, no one on earth who can "un-anoint" Saul. Instead, while he retains the character of a man permanently consecrated to God, God removes him from jurisdiction over the people of Israel. Saul is, as it were, a king without a kingdom. David's respect for Saul as the Lord's anointed is a testimony to David's faith in God, his hope in the permanency of God's actions, and the righteousness of his love for God and those whom God has consecrated to himself.

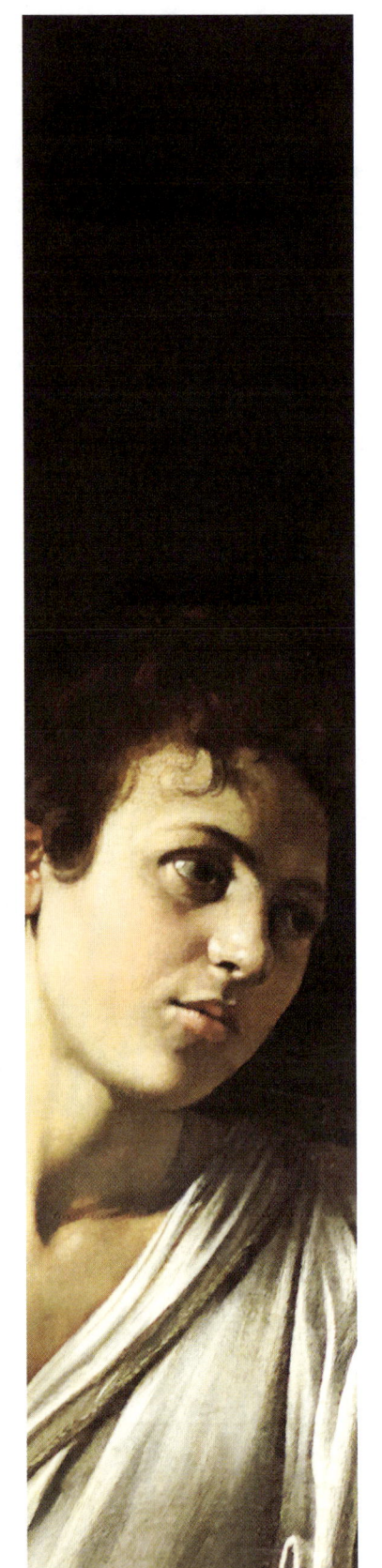

DAVID BECOMES KING OVER A UNITED ISRAEL

The death of Saul does not change the political landscape of Israel. The nation is as Saul left it: fragmented, ravaged by continual war with its neighbors, and roiled by continual internal political strife. As Bishop Barron describes, that is because Saul through his sins followed the devil, the "scatterer." So fragmented had the kingdom become that it nearly reverts to a federation of tribes, and David can only assume the kingship over his own tribe, the tribe of Judah (2 Sam 2:4).

One of the remaining sons of Saul, Ish-bosheth, assumes the kingship over the other eleven tribes (2 Sam 2:9). The reign of Ish-bosheth is short, however. Following a period of internal struggle between the followers of David and the followers of Ish-bosheth, Ish-bosheth is assassinated (2 Sam 4:7). This allows David to become king over an undivided Israel (2 Sam. 5:3).

With the death of Ish-bosheth, all twelve of the tribes gather at Hebron, which was the capital of Judah, and proclaim David king (2 Sam 5:1-5). From that point forward, David could have reigned over all Israel from Hebron. But David had a better idea that was as gracious as it was practical: he would establish a new capital for his kingdom in Jerusalem. The idea was gracious because Jerusalem is in the territory of the tribe of Benjamin, and so David's choice acknowledged the importance of Saul, who was a Benjaminite, as the Lord's first anointed king. The idea was practical because Jerusalem sits right near the border of the territory of Benjamin and the territory of Judah.

The only difficulty with establishing a capital in Jerusalem is that it was already inhabited. We are told in the book of Joshua that when the tribes were conquering the land of Canaan, "the Jebusites, the inhabitants of Jerusalem, the people of Judah could not drive out; so the Jebusites dwell with the people of Judah at Jerusalem to this day." (Josh 15:63)

The reason why the Judahites and the Benjaminites could not drive out the Jebusites was not a military one. True enough, Jerusalem was a military stronghold. But their failure was spiritual, not military.

> The anger of the LORD flared up against Israel, and he said: Because this nation has transgressed my covenant, which I enjoined on their ancestors, and has not listened to me, I for my part will not clear away for them any more of the nations Joshua left when he died. They will be made to test Israel, to see whether or not they will keep to the way of the LORD and continue in it as their ancestors did. (Judg 2:20-22)

The people's ability to take Jerusalem was a test of their spiritual faithfulness. In itself, the city is nearly impregnable; "but with God all things are possible" (Matt 19:26).

Amidst his spiritual strength, David finds the solution that had so long evaded the Israelites. Although the city could not be attacked from the outside, David advises his men to climb up the water shaft and to attack the city from the inside (2 Sam 5:8). As a sign of David's greater faithfulness than his forefathers, the Israelites are victorious almost instantly (1 Sam 5:9). David can now establish his capital as planned (2 Sam 5:12-16).

†

DAVID'S PRIESTHOOD AND THE LITURGICAL PROCESSION OF THE ARK

Bringing unity to the kingdom was not solely a matter of subduing its enemies to remove outward hostility. David also had to bring Israel inward peace through proper worship of the Lord. To seek this inward peace, David organized a liturgical procession in which the people carried the Ark of the Covenant to Jerusalem, so that they could place that great symbol of the Lord's presence among his people at the center of their kingdom.

The procession with the Ark was elaborate. As Bishop Barron observes, David assembled 30,000 men—the precise number previously lost by Saul—and together they processed "with songs and lyres and harps and tambourines and castanets and cymbals" (2 Sam 6:5). They proceeded in two stages. First, they brought it as far as Nacon. Here the procession comes to an abrupt halt. They are transporting it upon an ox-cart and one of the two men driving the cart, Uzzah, reaches out to steady the ark when an ox stumbles (2 Sam 6:6). God immediately strikes him dead (2 Sam 6:7). Out of fear, David abandons the procession for three months (2 Sam 6:9-11).

Although Second Samuel does not tell us why Uzzah died, First Chronicles does. Bishop Barron points out that God had originally established a Law for carrying the Ark in order to protect people from the consequence that Uzzah received. The Ark was to be carried

DAVID THE KING

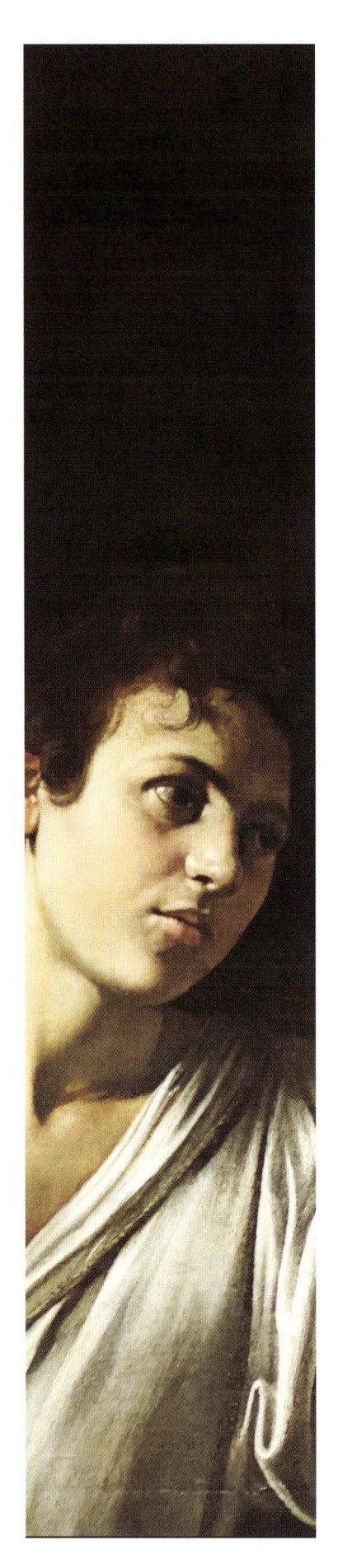

by poles that were fitted through its gilded rings (Exod 25:13-15). After the Golden Calf incident and the calling of the tribe of Levi to priestly service, the duty of carrying the Ark on those poles was given exclusively to the Levites (Deut. 10:8). After the death of Uzzah, David realizes that they have failed to observe these portions of the Law and he commands that they be observed in the future:

When the procession arrives in Jerusalem, David takes the ephod that Abiathar had given him and finally puts it on. "David was belted with a linen ephod…[and] David offered burnt offerings and peace offerings before the Lord. And when David had finished offering the burnt offerings and the peace offerings, he blessed the people in the name of the Lord of hosts" (2 Sam 6:14, 17-18).

David is dressing and acting like a priest—this should give us pause. Was it not the case that when Saul did the same thing, it was such a bad transgression that Saul had the kingdom taken from him?

The key difference between David and Saul is Jerusalem. Jerusalem, which many ancient commentators associate with the city of Salem mentioned in Genesis 14:18, was the ancient seat of the priest-king Melchizedek. Prior to David's conquest of Jerusalem, David comes close to acting like a priest a few times, but he never quite makes Saul's mistake of taking the priest's place:

- Twice he prays to God by means of the ephod, but without wearing it (1 Sam 23:10-12; 30:7-8).

- Once he eats the Bread of the Presence, which only priests may eat (1 Sam 21:3-6). Jesus seems to confirm that David was not yet a priest when he says that "it was not lawful for him to eat" it (Matt 12:4). Jesus also indicates that in this case the law was suspended by necessity.

Things change after David conquers Jerusalem. He inherits with the See of Jerusalem the ancient office of Melchizedek, and his sons serve as priests among the people in the order of Melchizedek (Ps 110:4; 2 Sam 8:18). The Letter to the Hebrews explains why:

> Now if perfection had been attainable through the Levitical priesthood (for under it the people received the law), what

further need would there have been for another priest to arise according to the order of Melchizedek, rather than one named according to the order of Aaron? For when there is a change in the priesthood, there is necessarily a change in the law as well. For the one of whom these things are spoken belonged to another tribe, from which no one has ever served at the altar. For it is evident that our Lord was descended from Judah, and in connection with that tribe Moses said nothing about priests. (Heb 7:11-14)

As Hebrews explains, the order of Melchizedek was necessary to overcome the shortcomings of Aaron's descendants (remember Eli, Phinehas, and Hophni?). In this way, David represents an initial fulfillment of God's promise to replace Eli with a faithful priest, even as Christ represents the ultimate fulfillment of that promise:

> Indeed, the law appoints men in their weakness as high priests, but the word of the oath [in Ps 110:4: "You are a priest forever according to the order of Melchizedek"], which came later than the law, appoints a Son who has been made perfect for ever. (Heb 7:28)

†

THE SPIRITUAL SENSES

In the allegorical sense, as Bishop Barron teaches, David represents Christ. He is motivated by love; he looks deeper than the surface and upon the heart; he loves his enemies; he turns the other cheek; and he tries to break the cycle of violence in Israel. Contrast David with Saul, who is a figure of Satan. He is motivated by envy; he relies on exterior appearances only; he hates his enemies; he retaliates; and he tries to continue the cycle of violence in Israel.

The outward conflict between Saul and David represents the inward conflict between two rival visions for humanity. Satan's vision is one that, as Bishop Barron explains, "scatters" people from one another by envy and violence, so that there is neither love nor peace among members of the human race. Christ's vision, by contrast, is one in which people are healed by grace, called to love and sacrifice according to the law of the gift, and so are knit into the unity of one body.

By providence, God takes Satan's envious action and turns it against him. God could annihilate Satan at any time, but God, like David, recognizes that "Not even the nature of the devil himself is evil, in so far as it is a nature" (Augustine, *City of God* 19.13). Acknowledging the goodness of creation, God prefers to work with it—even when that means bringing good out of evil—rather than destroying it (CCC 299, 312).

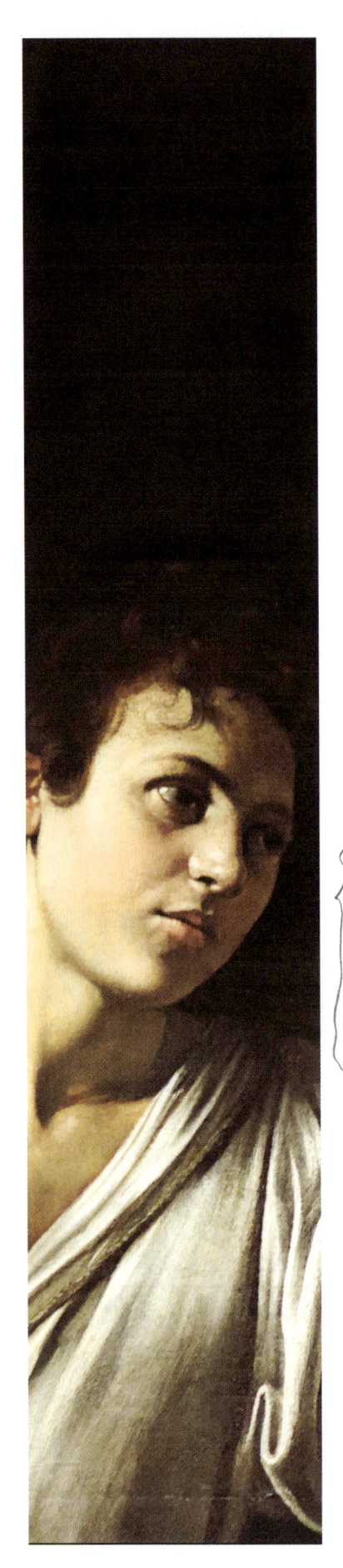

The transference of jurisdiction from Saul to David represents the coming of Christ into the world. When Christ comes into the world, he is king over it by right; he has, as it were, complete jurisdiction, while Satan has none. But that does not mean that everyone acknowledges Christ's jurisdiction. Just as the vast majority of people remained faithful to Saul, so the vast majority of people, upon the coming of Christ, knew nothing of him and paid no attention to him. Christ's reign on earth increases to the extent that he wins by his love an actual victory over souls (Thomas Aquinas, *ST*, IIIa, q. 59, a. 4; Leo XIII, *Annum Sacrum* 3-6). This victory is gradual, and its advancement is represented by the gradual manner in which David rallies people to himself.

The pinnacle of this drama is the cross, in which Christ, like David, destroys his enemy's evil without destroying his enemy. David conquers Saul not by fighting against him, but by *not fighting for him*. Saul needs David to be victorious against the Philistines, but David is too busy making reparation for Saul's evil—represented by the Amalekites—to fight for Saul. Similarly, Christ is victorious on the cross not by warring directly against Satan, but by not fighting for him. On the cross, Christ chooses the nonviolent path of loving and forgiving his enemies and making reparation for the sins of us all.

Out of Christ's victory arose Pentecost and the birth of the Church, which is "the kingdom of Christ now present in mystery" (LG 3). The birth of the Church is prefigured by the coalescence of Israelites around David, what Bishop Barron calls "the mystical body of David." The mystical body of David is the union of the tribes around him, beginning with Judah—which represents the Jewish people—and extending ultimately to the other tribes.

When we are brought into the Church, we come to know Christ not only as our king but also as our great high priest (Heb 4:14). For this reason it is fitting that once David becomes king over Israel, he assumes the role of priest-king, which he inherits from the office of Melchizedek. As priest, David leads the people of Israel in the sacrificial service of the Lord, through which they are knit into one body united in right praise. Christ accomplishes the same thing more fully. He offers himself once for all on the cross—a sacrifice that he renews daily through the Eucharist—and so knits people by his infinite charity into the mystical body of the Church (CCC 1544-45).

As a sign and symbol of what happens when we are invited into Christ's mystical body, we have the procession of the Ark into Jerusalem. The Ark, as Bishop Barron explains, prefigures Mary (CCC 2676). David used the same language about the Ark as St. Elizabeth used about Mary at the Visitation. But understanding the journey of the Ark is difficult on account of Uzzah, who reaches out his hand to steady the Ark and is struck dead. While we should rightly wonder with Bishop Barron about the mystery of Uzzah's death in the literal sense, we can at least see Uzzah in the allegorical sense as a figure of Peter. Uzzah, like Peter, is eager to follow the Lord and so journeys together with the Ark of the Covenant as close as can be. But just like Uzzah moved the Ark on his own terms rather than on God's terms, so likewise Peter initially wanted to journey with Mary towards Jesus on his own terms. Peter wanted Christ without the cross; he rebuked Christ in anticipation of the cross (Matt 16:22), and then fled and denied Christ when it came time for the cross (Matt 26:69-75). The carrying of the Ark by the Levites represents Peter's rehabilitation by Christ after the Resurrection (John 21:15-19). At this point, Peter has been ordained a priest himself (John 20:22-23), and he agrees to pick up his cross and follow Christ on Christ's terms.

In the tropological sense, the struggle between Saul and David represents the struggle of two rival kings over our souls. Each of us faces the temptation to act like Saul—to rule ourselves on our own terms, to live in envy of the good God does for others, to dwell only in the world of exterior appearances and pleasures, to return evil for evil, and so to continue the cycle of violence in the world. Only if we are centered on Christ and knit by his love and grace into his mystical body, the Church, can we break out of that cycle, live by love, dwell in the world of the heart, and so help bring about God's nonviolent kingdom on earth.

Our principle challenge, as Bishop Barron describes, is the challenge faced by Peter: do we want to follow Christ on our own terms or will we follow Christ on his terms? Following Christ on his terms means picking up our cross. It means loving our enemies, praying for those who persecute us (Matt 5:44). In the anagogical sense, it means being so busy about the business of overcoming evil with love that we defeat Satan in our lives precisely by *not fighting for him*. Then, as Bishop Barron points out, when Christ is the center of our lives we partake of a loving unity that compels people to it by the power of its own desirability. In this way, as we become woven more deeply into the fabric of the mystical body of Christ, our very lives become a powerful evangelistic witness and we draw others to Christ, just as David by his faithfulness to the Lord drew all Israel to himself.

DAVID THE KING

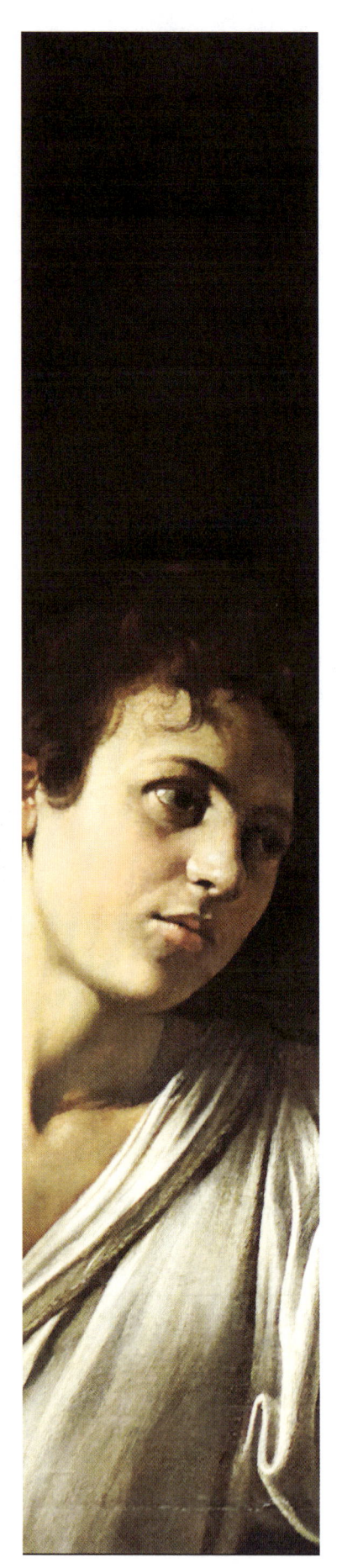

QUESTIONS FOR UNDERSTANDING

1. Why is Saul envious of David? How does Saul's envy contribute to David's rise? (1 Sam 18:6-9, 25-30; 19:1-2, 11-12, 18-24)

2. Why won't David kill Saul, and why does David kill the man who claims to have done so? (1 Sam 24:5-8; 26:8-11; 31:1-4; 2 Sam 1:6-10, 13-16)

3. How and why did David establish his capital in Jerusalem? (Judg 2:20-23; 2 Sam 5:6-12)

4. Why does David not put on the ephod until after he conquers Jerusalem? How does the fact that David is king but also becomes a priest affect the Levitical priesthood? (Gen 14:18; 2 Sam 6:14, 17-18; Ps 110:1-4; 2 Sam 8:18; Heb 7:11-14; CCC 1539)

5. Who ultimately fulfills the prophecy "You are a priest forever according to the order of Melchizedek"? (Ps 110:4) What can we expect to gain from this great high priest? (Heb 7:22-27; CCC 1544)

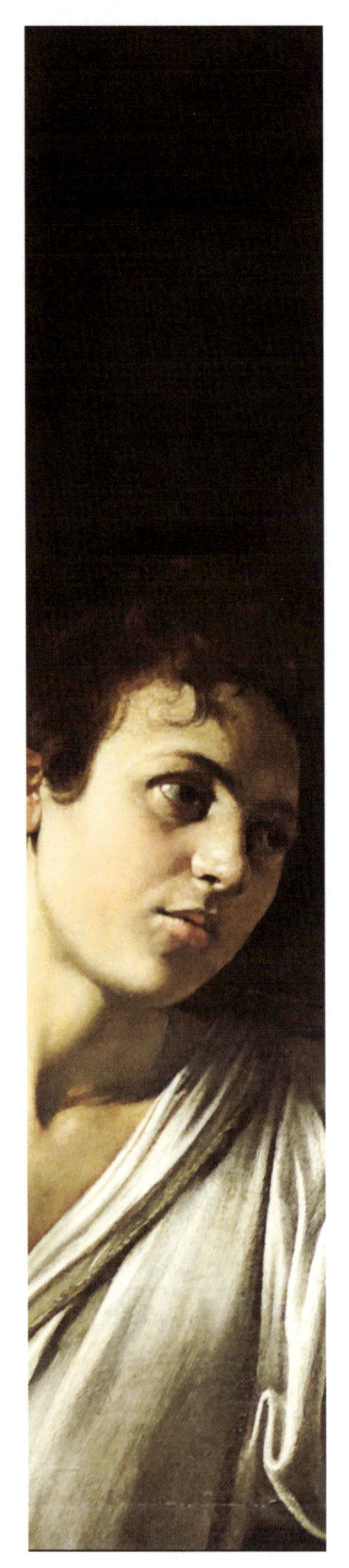

QUESTIONS FOR APPLICATION

1. Think of a time when you had to confront evil in your life. How can David be a model of how to deal with evil?

2. Is there a situation in your life right now where you are struggling to follow Christ on Christ's terms? How can the story of Uzzah help you through it?

3. What are some areas in which our contemporary culture focuses on outward appearances? How does the teaching of the Church help us see the heart of the matter?

DAVID THE KING

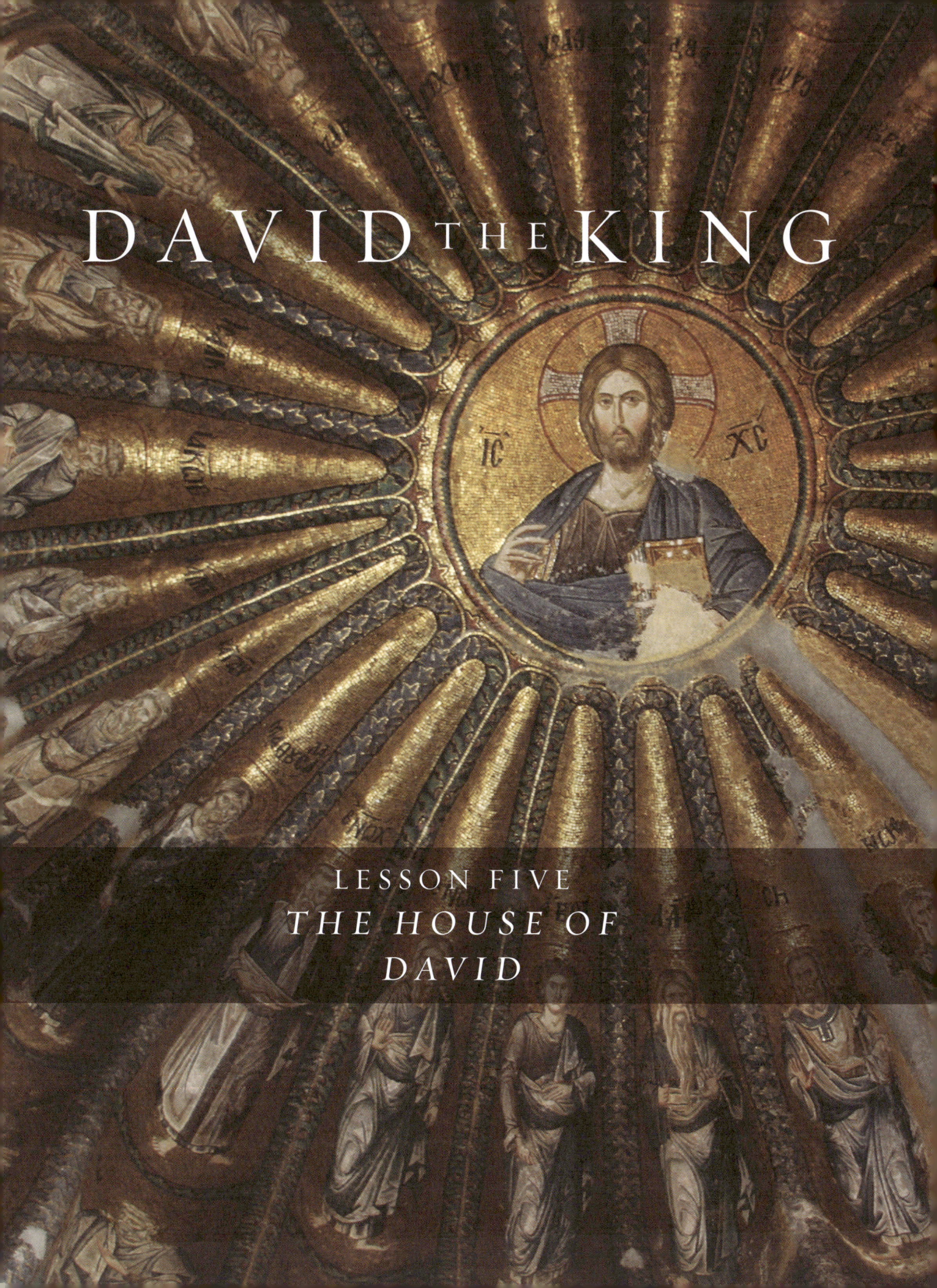

LESSON FIVE
THE HOUSE OF DAVID

LESSON FIVE IMAGE
The Genealogy of Jesus. Mosaic.
Chora Church. Istanbul, Turkey.

THE HOUSE OF DAVID
LESSON FIVE OUTLINE

I. THE DAVIDIC COVENANT (2 Sam 7:1-17)
   A. David is given a time of rest from his enemies
      1. Sabbath rest
      2. Time of right praise
   B. David wants to build a Temple for the Ark
   C. God says "no" but promises to build an everlasting "house" for David
      1. Dynasty
      2. Anticipates the mystical body of Christ
   D. Text written during Babylonian Captivity
      1. David's line destroyed
      2. Israel still trusts in the power of God

II. JESUS, THE FULFILLMENT OF THE DAVIDIC COVENANT
   A. Genealogy in Matthew and Luke (three sets of 14)
   B. Son of David
   C. Jesus said "the kingdom of God is at hand"
   D. Bartimaeus: healing and dancing behind Jesus as he goes into Jerusalem
   E. A new Temple built by Jesus to replace the old
   F. The Church, the mystical body of Christ
      1. Where Jesus has reigned for 2,000 years
      2. "Gates of hell won't prevail against it"
   G. Eternal kingship of the Son of David

DAVID THE KING

LESSON FIVE

THE HOUSE OF DAVID

In the fifth talk, Bishop Barron unpacks the Christological significance of the Davidic Covenant, that special relationship which God establishes with David and his successors in 2 Samuel 7. Since this talk concerns only one chapter of Scripture, Bishop Barron is able to take some time to give us a helpful review of the context in which scholars believe it to have been written, as well as to delve more deeply into the spiritual significance of the text.

THE CONTEXT

Let's begin by reviewing the context of 2 Samuel 7. More broadly speaking, as Bishop Barron described in Lesson 1, most scholars believe that 1-2 Samuel was originally part of an organic whole, the Deuteronomistic History. The Deuteronomistic History is thought to have been written either during or just after the Babylonian Captivity in the mid-500s BC as a means of explaining theologically and historically how the people from the Kingdom of Judah had incurred the Deuteronomistic curse for breaking the Deuteronomistic Covenant, and what the Lord's consequences were for doing so.

More immediately speaking, as Bishop Barron described in Lesson 4, 2 Samuel 7 follows upon David's consolidation of the kingdom. After a long struggle with Saul, in which God providentially turned Saul's envy into a confirmation of David's kingship, David became king over all Israel, conquered Jerusalem, and established Jerusalem as his capital. The conquering of Jerusalem had a threefold significance: in terms of the Mosaic Covenant, it represented the first time that anyone in Israel has been faithful enough to God that he might allow them to conquer this nearly impregnable military stronghold; in terms of politics, it represented a gracious move on David's part to locate the capital of the kingdom in the territory of Saul's tribe, the tribe of

Benjamin, rather than David's tribe, the tribe of Judah; in terms of theology, it represented David's assumption of the priesthood of Melchizedek, the ancient priest-king from Genesis 14.

†

THE LITERAL SENSE

"Rest from Your Enemies Round About"

We begin 2 Samuel 7 with God giving David "rest from all his enemies round about" (2 Sam 7:1). These words are full of significance in the Deuteronomistic History. They represent the fulfillment of God's charge to the Israelites to cast out idolatry from the land and of God's promise to reward the Israelites for doing so. Here is what God had commanded and promised in the Book of Deuteronomy:

> These are the statutes and ordinances which you must be careful to observe in the land which the LORD, the God of your ancestors, has given you to possess, throughout the time you live on its soil. Destroy entirely all the places where the nations you are to dispossess serve their gods, on the high mountains, on the hills, and under every green tree. Tear down their altars, smash their sacred pillars, burn up their asherahs, and chop down the idols of their gods, that you may destroy the very name of them from that place. After you have crossed the Jordan and dwell in the land which the LORD, your God, is giving you as a heritage, *when he has given you rest from all your enemies round about* and you live there in security, then to the place which the LORD, your God, chooses as the dwelling place for his name you shall bring all that I command you: your burnt offerings and sacrifices, your tithes and personal contributions, and every special offering you have vowed to the LORD. You shall rejoice in the presence of the LORD, your God, with your sons and daughters, your male and female slaves, as well as with the Levite within your gates, who has no hereditary portion with you. (Deut 12:1-3, 10-12; emphasis added)

©2017 Word on Fire Catholic Ministries

Notice how God uses that very same language "rest from all your enemies round about," as an important part of his plan for the people of Israel. The first half of the Deuteronomistic History, up through the reign of Saul, is the drama of how Israel did *not* do what the Lord had asked and so did not receive that rest. One instance of that failure was leaving the Jebusites in Jerusalem; another was Saul's refusal to put the Amalekites to the ban (remember how that came back to haunt him?). There were other failures. Practically every tribe left at least one foreign nation with foreign gods to dwell in its midst. The Book of Judges details a litany of these refusals to "do battle with evil all the way down," to use Bishop Barron's words.

The only way the Israelites were going to get *rest from their enemies* was if they returned to the radical faithfulness mandated in the Book of Deuteronomy. We can see here an echo of a call to repentance and faithfulness in the midst of the Babylonian Captivity, a glimmer of hope that the people might turn again and be restored to their former dependence on God and independence from secular nations.

We heard in Lesson 4 how David represents that radical faithfulness. As a figure of Christ, he shows us how clinging to the Lord with the heart that empowers a person to overcome the deepest and darkest of evils, no matter how large they may seem. We also saw how the story of David anticipates the story of Christ right up through outpouring of the Holy Spirit at Pentecost. In this lesson, we see that Christological progression continue. Just as the Holy Spirit pours out upon the Church "the unity of the Spirit in the bond of peace" (Eph 4:3) and forms the Church thereby into the mystical body of Christ, so likewise the formation of what Bishop Barron calls "the mystical body of David" in the second half of First Samuel and the beginning of Second Samuel anticipates the establishment of a Spirit-centered peace being poured out upon the land.

The reception of that peace was tied to the conquest of Jerusalem. Notice how Deuteronomy had stipulated that Israelites should "seek the place which the Lord your God will choose out of all your tribes to put his name and make his habitation there." That place was Jerusalem, whose very name is derived from the Hebrew word for peace, *Shalom*. Previously, both Judah and Benjamin had failed to conquer Jerusalem, and so the entire people of Israel had been denied the peace of that city. When David finally conquers it, not only does David inherit the city's office of priest-king, the people themselves inherit the peace that follows from liturgical communion with the Lord, which David establishes by faithfully carrying out his office.

DAVID THE KING

The Lord's House and David's House

If the strength of the kingdom was in its relationship with the Lord, then the historical events surrounding the consolidation of the kingdom might seem somewhat backwards. First the royal palace is built; then David's family is established; only then is the Temple of the Lord built. Should it not be the other way around?

We read just after the conquest of Jerusalem:

> Hiram, king of Tyre, sent envoys to David along with cedar wood, and carpenters and masons, who built a house for David. David now knew that the LORD had truly established him as king over Israel and had exalted his kingdom for the sake of his people Israel. David took more concubines and wives in Jerusalem after he had come from Hebron, and more sons and daughters were born to him. (2 Sam 5:11-13)

After the construction of his house, David became, as Bishop Barron explained in the previous talk, a *paterfamilias*. *Paterfamilias* is a Latin term that means "father of the family." It was a technical term in Roman law and philosophy describing the male head of a great household, who possessed ultimate legal authority over his immediate and extended family, their servants, and their property. With the establishment of this great house, David now becomes what the people had hoped Saul would become: a glamorous figurehead, who by his grandeur and magnanimity can represent the greatness of the people (see 1 Sam 8:19-20).

God grants the favor to David of becoming what Israel longed for, but that favor came with a strong temptation to pride. God had brought David from a small shepherd boy to a great king; David now has to contend with the temptation to forget that the Lord is the basis of all his greatness, and that the Lord has exalted the kingdom not for David's sake, but "for the sake of *his* [i.e., God's] people Israel." The fact that David's actions are in the order of 1) house 2) family 3) God is an early warning sign that David's rise to power is also going to become an occasion of sin.

The disorder of David's actions does eventually prick his conscience. He goes to the Prophet Nathan, who succeeds to Samuel's office as David's advisor, and mentions the matter to him (2 Sam 7:2). Nathan, still evidently a bit new at his job, tells David, "Go, do all that is in your heart; for the Lord is with you" (2 Sam 7:3). But that night the Lord corrects Nathan and tells him to go back and forbid David to build the house. As Bishop Barron points out, the Lord forbids David to build a temple for the Lord because David had spent too much time at war: "You have shed much blood and have waged great wars; you shall not build a house to my name, because you have shed so much blood before me upon the earth" (1 Chron 22:8).

Later David's son, Solomon, will build a house for the Lord. In the meantime, the Lord finds two other ways to reward David's faithfulness.

First, the Lord promises to give the Israelites *rest from all their enemies round about*. This is the culmination of the promise made in Deuteronomy 12 quoted above. The Lord confirms that David is the first leader of Israel since the time they inherited the Promised Land to receive the rest promised in Deuteronomy as a reward for faithfulness to the covenant with God.

Second, the Lord promises to build David a house. Of course, David already has a palace that he received from the King of Tyre. But, as Bishop Barron clarifies, the Lord is speaking of a royal house, a dynastic line, which will extend in perpetuity. Unlike the previous reward, this reward has no antecedent promise in Deuteronomy. It was an entirely gratuitous addition to previous promises—a fantastic, almost unbelievable gift, as Bishop Barron observes.

The promise was almost unbelievable for two reasons. On a basic level, the world has never known a perpetual dynastic line. Most dynastic lines rise and fall within a few hundred years. In the West, for example, the longest dynastic line was that of the Capetians, who reigned on the French throne from 987–1328, a mere 341 years. On a more contextual level, as Bishop Barron describes, the promise was even more incredible because of the situation in which scholars believe it to have been written. For the Deuteronomistic Historian to record this particular promise during or just after the period of the Babylonian Captivity would have required a robust and confident sense of hope in the Lord to bring about what seemed outwardly impossible.

If we return to the passage in First Chronicles that describes the reason why the Lord forbade David to build the temple, we can find out a little something more about why 2 Samuel 7 gave the people of Israel hope during the Babylonian Captivity. When David was recounting the story to his son and successor, Solomon, he describes God's second promise in these words:

> A son will be born to you. He will be a peaceful man, and I will give him rest from all his enemies on every side. For Solomon shall be his name, and in his time I will bestow peace and tranquility on Israel. It is he who shall build a house for my name; he shall be a son to me, and I will be a father to him, and I will establish the throne of his kingship over Israel forever.
> (1 Chron 22:9-10)

Let us note for now that these are not the words that Nathan spoke *verbatim*; this is David recalling the words that Nathan spoke and summarizing them for Solomon. In doing so, David fills in a certain "blank spot" in Nathan's prophecy. Nathan says a lot of things about the prophesied son that align with what Scripture tells us elsewhere. But Nathan never said "the son I am talking about is Solomon." David adds that detail because it seemed so obvious to him. The people of Israel followed him in that interpretation, understanding God's promise to refer to Solomon.

Seeing the promised son as Solomon gave the people of Israel a reason to hope. By the time of the Babylonian Captivity, they could see in hindsight that Solomon had apparently satisfied all of the criteria of Nathan's prophecy in 2 Samuel 7:

> "I will raise up your offspring after you, who shall come forth from your body" (fulfilled in 2 Sam 12:24)
> "I will establish his kingdom" (fulfilled in 1 Kings 1:39)
> "He shall build a house for my name" (fulfilled in 1 Kings 6)

For this reason, the people could look to the history of Solomon's rule as a fulfillment of the prophecy confirming God's promise of an everlasting line to David.

The confidence of the tradition is reflected in the Psalms, which Bishop Barron references for us:

> For your merciful love was established for ever,
> your faithfulness is firm as the heavens.
> You have said, "I have made a covenant with my chosen one,
> I have sworn to David my servant:
> 'I will establish your descendants for ever,
> and build your throne for all generations.' " (Ps 89:2-4)

©2017 Word on Fire Catholic Ministries

> The Lord swore to David a sure oath
> from which he will not turn back:
> "One of the sons of your body
> I will set on your throne.
> If your sons keep my covenant
> and my testimonies which I shall teach them,
> their sons also for ever
> shall sit upon your throne." (Ps 132:11-12)

The people in the Babylonian Captivity, like the Psalmist, looked to God's promise to David as a sure foundation from which they could hope for the renewal of Israel. It may have been true that in the past God had taken away the priesthood from Eli and the kingship from Saul, but God had sworn an oath to David that things would be different this time. Even if the restoration of the Davidic dynasty seemed well neigh impossible, if the people could find even a sliver of trust in God, they could—and did—latch onto God's promise to David confirmed by the events of Solomon's life as a sure sign that God had not and would not forsake them forever.

†

THE SPIRITUAL SENSES

Solomon and the Promised King

Were David and the people of Israel correct to identify the promised successor to David as Solomon? Perhaps. The similarities between the promised successor and Solomon are undeniable. But let us recall that when Nathan uttered his prophecy, Solomon had not even been born. Nathan knew nothing more about Solomon when he uttered that prophecy than David did, because no one knew anything about Solomon! All that Nathan knew was that he was faithfully transmitting the word of the Lord to refer to *some* descendent of David. The fact that David and the people of Israel later associated that descendent with Solomon was a matter of interpretation.

St. Augustine wasn't so sure that David had gotten things right. Reading the words of Nathan in 2 Samuel 7:12 very closely, there was one little detail that stuck out to him. Here is that verse again:

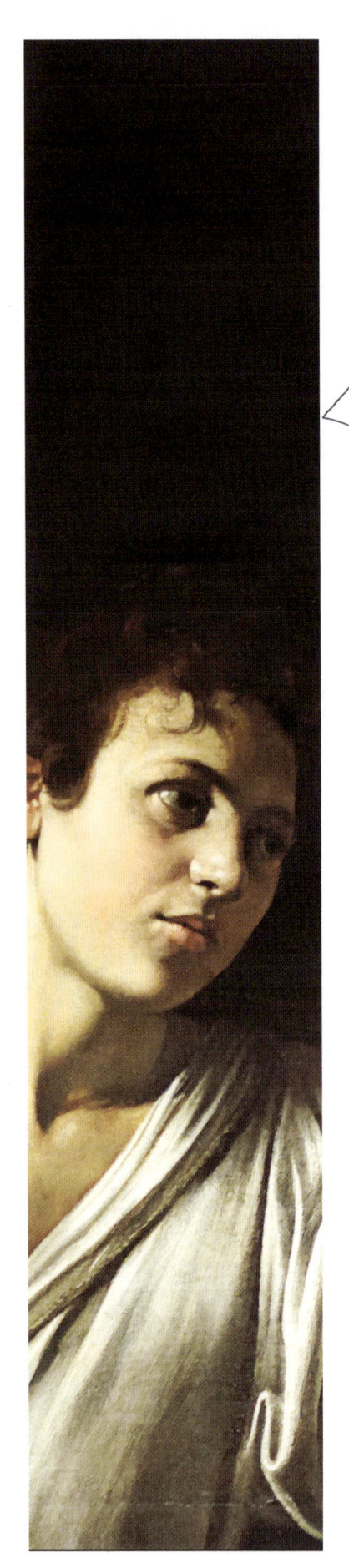

> When your days have been completed and you rest with your ancestors, I will raise up your offspring after you, sprung from your loins, and I will establish his kingdom.

The grammar of the sentence clearly implies a sequence in time:

1) David's days are fulfilled
2) David lies down with his fathers (that is, he dies)
3) God raises up David's offspring and establish his kingdom

The difficulty that St. Augustine had was that the actual sequence of events narrated in the Deuteronomistic History followed a different progression:

1) David's days were fulfilled
2) David appointed Solomon as his successor
3) David died

Here is how the story went. When David was old and it seemed clear that he was going to die, David's fourth son, Adonijah, thought he would attempt to seize the kingdom (1 Kings 1:5). In order to prevent a *coup d'état*, Solomon's mother, Bathsheba, asked David to formally name Solomon as his successor (1 Kings 1:20). David—of his own initiative—decided to have Solomon anointed early. That is to say that, unlike the promised successor that Nathan describes, Solomon was anointed king over Israel *before* David died, not afterwards (1 Kings 1:34). Consequently, Augustine concludes, this promise cannot refer to Solomon (*City of God* 17.8.2).

St. Augustine thought that God, in his providence knowing how close the similarities would be between the promised king and Solomon, permitted this unusual historical event precisely so that we would *not* associate the promise with Solomon. On the contrary, St. Augustine would have us read the prophecy as referring to Christ rather than to Solomon, without suggesting the least change in Nathan's intention.

©2017 Word on Fire Catholic Ministries

SOLOMON

Solomon, whose name is related to the word for "peace," is the second son of David and Bathsheba, and the initial heir to David's throne. From his birth, Solomon is marked as beloved by God. David, believing him to be the promised faithful heir to the Davidic Covenant, names Solomon his successor.

Initially, Solomon's kingship is a mirror of David's fidelity. When the Lord visits him and promises to grant him one wish, he prays only for wisdom to govern the people of the Lord well. God promises as a reward for this holy request to make Solomon great in temporal wealth and power, as well as in wisdom.

At the height of his wealth and power, Solomon fulfills God's plan to build the Temple. The Temple is a magnificent structure, set on dressed stones, built with costly lumber, and entirely overlaid with gold. However, just as David initially paid more attention to his own house (though he later realized this and corrected himself), so also does Solomon spends more time and money on his own house than on the house of the Lord (Solomon does not correct himself like David).

Following the building of the Temple, Solomon succumbs to similar temptations as had David, only on a much greater scale. The Lord warns him not to take any foreign wives, for fear that by his delight in them he will be led to worship foreign gods. But Solomon does not listen; he takes seven hundred wives and three hundred concubines, and ends up following them in the worship of their foreign gods.

As a result of Solomon's idolatry, the Lord inflicts a similar punishment on Solomon as he had on Saul. However, he mitigates the punishment in two ways. First, the Lord does not take the kingdom away from Solomon directly; the kingdom is to be taken from his son, Rehoboam. Second, the Lord does not take the entire kingdom away; he allows the tribe of Judah to remain, together with the tribe of Benjamin.

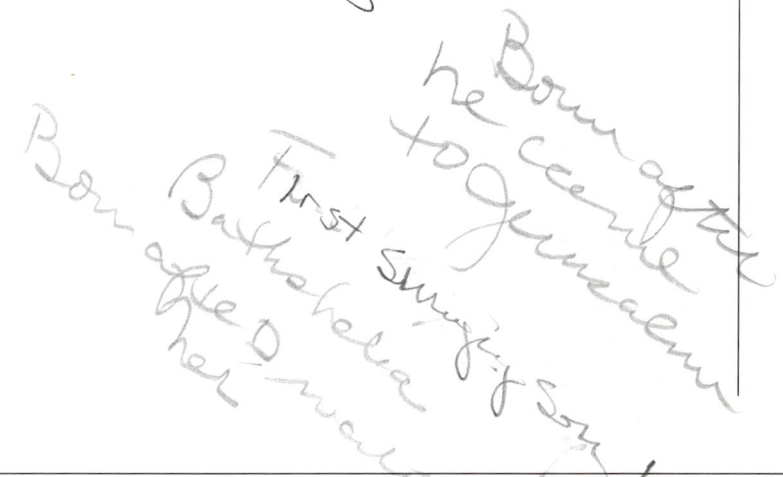

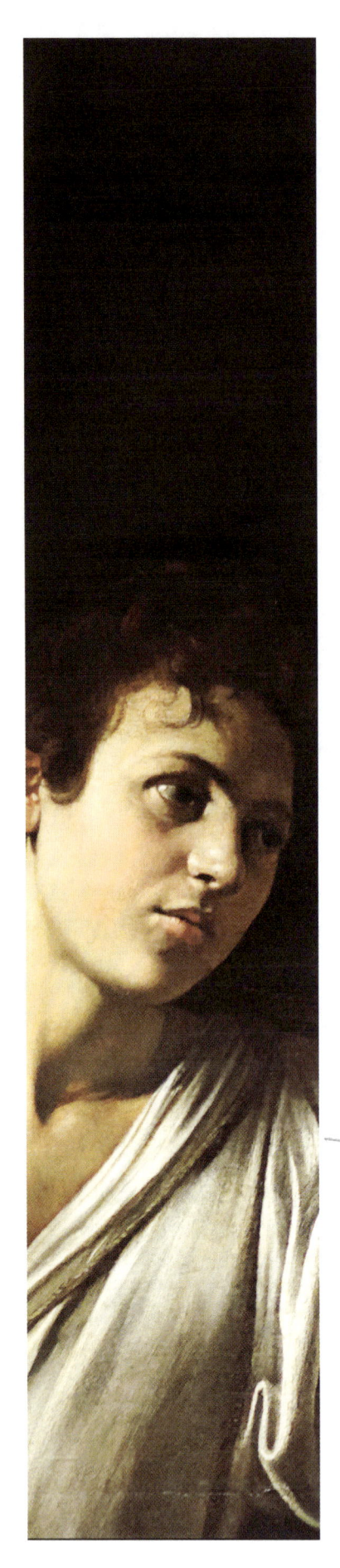

Jesus and the Promised King

The two Gospels that record Jesus' genealogy and his birth, Matthew and Luke, both give a Christological interpretation of the promise made to David, rather than a Solomonic one.

Matthew's Gospel starts off by announcing Jesus' Davidic credentials in the very first sentence (Matt 1:1). From there, the Evangelist gives us a genealogy that goes from Abraham to Jesus, divided into three groups of fourteen ancestors: Abraham to David, David to the Babylonian Captivity, and the Babylonian Captivity to Jesus. Since Matthew, like any other inspired author of Scripture, is a real author in every sense of the word, the groups give us a sense of what he thought mattered most to his audience. Even five centuries later, the two main things on the mind of the people of Israel as they awaited the fulfillment of God's promises were David and the Babylonian Captivity.

Part of the reason why the Babylonian Captivity mattered to the people of Israel all those years later was that they had never quite recovered from it. Their ancestral land had been under a near-continuous succession of foreign overlords ever since: the Babylonians (586BC-538BC), the Medo-Persians (538BC-333BC), the Macedonians (333BC-323BC), the Ptolomies (323BC-198BC), the Seleucids (198BC-110BC), and then—following a brief period of self-rule under the Hasmoneans (110BC-63BC), who were not heirs to the throne of David—the Romans (63BC-637AD). In the midst of this near-continuous domination by foreign powers, the Davidic line faded somewhat into the background. The last recorded heir to David in the Old Testament is Zerubbabel, who oversaw the rebuilding of the Temple after the return from Babylon (Haggai 1:1). This means that the official royal lineage of David effectively "dropped off the map" after the return from Babylon.

To a first-century Jewish reader, then, the most important question to ask about Jesus would have been, "how do we get from Zerubbabel to Jesus"? Matthew gives us that answer:

> Zerubbabel the father of Abiud. Abiud became the father of Eliakim, Eliakim the father of Azor, Azor the father of Zadok. Zadok became the father of Achim, Achim the father of Eliud,

©2017 Word on Fire Catholic Ministries

> Eliud the father of Eleazar. Eleazar became the father of Matthan, Matthan the father of Jacob, Jacob the father of Joseph, the husband of Mary. Of her was born Jesus who is called the Messiah. (Matt 1:13-16)

As a confirmation of this royal pedigree, Bishop Barron describes how Matthew puts within his genealogy a little numerical code. In Hebrew, each of the letters of the alphabet has a number associated with it, because Hebrew does not have a separate system for writing numbers the way that English does. Given that Hebrew has a different letter order than English, and that it uses no vowels, the three letters for David, D-V-D, correspond with the numbers 4 + 6 + 4. If you add that up, the result is 14. Matthew's three groups of fourteen proclaim to us the primary truth that the genealogy is intended to convey: Jesus is "David! David! David!"

Luke's Gospel also affirms Jesus' Davidic identity, although it does so in a somewhat different way. Instead of giving us his royal pedigree from the start (he does this later in Luke 3:23-38), Luke records the witness of two important figures, both of whom give testimony to Jesus' Davidic ancestry: the archangel Gabriel (Luke 1:32-33), and John the Baptist's father, Zechariah (Luke 1:67-72); he also references historical records (Luke 2:4-5).

Given the fact that David himself had interpreted Nathan's prophecy as referring to Solomon, and that the Solomonic interpretation had been an important support to the people of Israel in the period during and after the Babylonian Captivity, it would take a lot of authority to tip the balance of interpretation towards the vision that St. Augustine would later represent. Luke is ready for the challenge. As a good historian, he lines up supporting documentation for his claim: angelic authority, prophetic authority, and documentary authority.

The angelic authority comes to us in the moment of the Annunciation. As Bishop Barron quotes, the Archangel Gabriel declares:

> He will be great and will be called Son of the Most High, and the Lord God will give him the throne of David his father, and he will rule over the house of Jacob forever, and of his kingdom there will be no end. (Luke 1:32-33)

This is a direct reference to Nathan's prophecy in 2 Samuel 7, phrased in almost the same language. It is a confirmation—equal in significance to that of Matthew's genealogy—that the child to be born of Mary is the descendent who will sit upon the throne of David perpetually.

The angelic authority is confirmed by prophetic authority under Zechariah. Zechariah is John the Baptist's father. After the miraculous birth of John, we are told that Zachariah "was filled with the Holy Spirit, and prophesied" (Luke 1:67). His prophecy takes the form of the song known in the liturgy as the *Benedictus*, which the Church sings in her public prayer each day at Morning Prayer.

> Blessed be the Lord, the God of Israel, for he has visited and brought redemption to his people. He has raised up a horn for our salvation within the house of David his servant, even as he promised through the mouth of his holy prophets from of old: salvation from our enemies and from the hand of all who hate us. (Luke 1:68-71)

The prophetic authority is confirmed by historical, documentary authority. In the second chapter of his Gospel, Luke tells us that the Roman Emperor, Caesar Augustus, had decreed a census (Luke 2:1). Scholars dispute the exact nature of the census, but suffice it to say that the Israelites had to return to their ancestral villages to be counted. Joseph, we are told, "went up… to Judea," that is, to the land of David's tribe, the tribe of Judah, "to the city of David, which is called Bethlehem, because he was of the house and lineage of David" (Luke 2:4). Although we no longer possess the records of that census, in the first century Joseph's enrollment at Bethlehem could be taken as formal Roman administrative confirmation of the Davidic lineage of the family into which Jesus was born.

Jesus, the Temple, and the Kingdom

Just as Jesus transforms the meaning of the promise of a king to reign over God's people, so likewise does he transform the meaning of the Temple to be built and the kingdom to be established by that king.

As the Davidic heir, one of Jesus' tasks was to "build a house" for the Lord. The Solominic interpretation of those words held that the task of the Davidic heir was to complete the Temple so as to replace the Tabernacle. Of course, by Jesus' time the Temple had already been built (and rebuilt!). But Jesus gives us a different understanding of the words. Upon going into the temple to cleanse it, Jesus argues with the Temple officials about the very meaning of the "Temple" about which Nathan spoke.

He made a whip out of cords and drove them all out of the temple area, with the sheep and oxen, and spilled the coins of the money-changers and overturned their tables, and to those who sold doves he said, "Take these out of here, and stop making my Father's house a marketplace." His disciples recalled the words of scripture, "Zeal for your house will consume me." At this the Jews answered and said to him, "What sign can you show us for doing this?" Jesus answered and said to them, "Destroy this temple and in three days I will raise it up." The Jews said, "This temple has been under construction for forty-six years,* and you will raise it up in three days?" *But he was speaking about the temple of his body.* (John 2:15-21; emphasis added)

According to Jesus, the Temple spoken about in 2 Samuel 7 is not the building that Solomon built in Jerusalem and that was rebuilt under Zerubbabel after the Babylonian Captivity; it is instead Jesus' own body, which was destroyed in the Crucifixion, but raised up again on the third day. Moreover, as St. Paul tells us, the Church is incorporated by the Eucharist into that body and so can rightly be said to *be* that body (1 Cor 11-12). The establishment of the Church is an extension of Nathan's prophecy about the Temple.

The fulfillment of Nathan's prophecy about the Temple points us to the fulfillment of Nathan's prophecy about the kingdom. As the Second Vatican Council teaches, precisely in virtue of the fact that the Church is the Body of Christ, the Church is also the nucleus of Christ's reign on earth. It is "the kingdom of Christ now present in mystery" (LG 3).

As Bishop Barron explains, when Jesus promised to Peter that the Church would be established forever, "and the gates of the netherworld shall not prevail against it" (Matt 16:18), Jesus was not, as it were, promising anything new. He was merely confirming and explaining the original promise he intended to fulfill: the promise to "establish his kingdom forever" (2 Sam 7:13). In other words, just as the son promised to David is fulfilled by Christ, so likewise the kingdom promised to David's son is fulfilled by the Church. It may be that there are many similarities between the things Nathan promised and the things Solomon did. But with angelic, prophetic, historical, and divine authority, the Gospels proclaim even better news: God never did forget his people; he continued actively among them, preparing them ceaselessly for the fulfillment of his promises to them. The Israelites were right to look with David at 2 Samuel 7 for consolation. But in the fullness of time, the fulfillment of that consolation in Jesus was more radical, more powerful, and more transformative than they ever could have imagined.

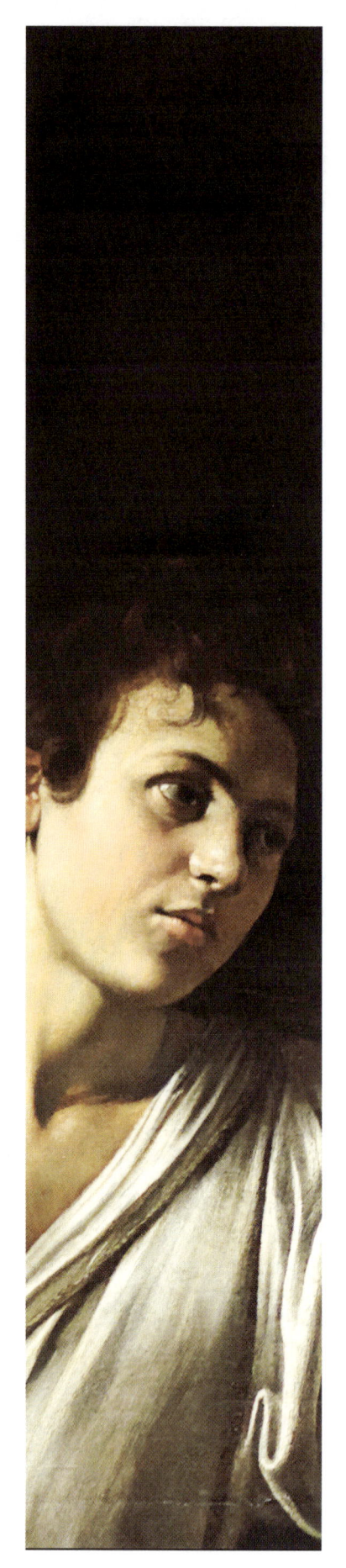

QUESTIONS FOR UNDERSTANDING

1. What is the Davidic Covenant revealed in Nathan's prophecy? (2 Sam 7:1-16) Why does God grant David "a rest from his enemies"? (Deut 12:1-12)

2. Why doesn't David get to build the Temple in Jerusalem? (2 Sam 7:12-15; 1 Chron 22:8)

3. Why would people in the time of the Babylonian Captivity write about God's promises to David? (1 Chron 22:9-10; 2 Sam 12:24; 1 Kings 1:39; 1 Kings 6:1).

4. Why do we believe, as did St. Augustine, that the promise of a perpetual heir in the Davidic Covenant refers to Jesus? (Matt 1:1-17; Luke 1:32-33, 67-72; 2:1-5)

QUESTIONS FOR APPLICATION

1. How could a "passion for the impossible" help you ask God for what you or your community need right now?

2. Has there ever been some situation in your life in which you, like the Israelites, were being "held captive" from a better relationship with God? How can thinking about salvation history help you see God at work in your life during those times?

3. How can the story of David help us deepen our devotion to the Church?

4. Think about Augustine's interpretation of the Davidic Covenant for a moment. Has there ever been a situation in your life when you thought that God was doing one thing, but when you looked at it very carefully later on, he turned out to be doing something very different (and perhaps even better!)? If so, please describe.

DAVID THE KING

LESSON SIX
ABSALOM, MY SON!

LESSON SIX IMAGE

King David in Prayer. Pieter de Grebber, 1635-40.
Utrecht, Museum Catharijneconvent.

ABSALOM, MY SON!
LESSON SIX OUTLINE

I. THE SWORD NEVER LEAVES DAVID'S HOUSE
   A. Bathsheba incident
   B. Serious sins of adultery and murder

II. DAVID'S CHILDREN: TAMAR, AMNON, AND ABSALOM
   A. Amnon lusts after his half-sister, Tamar, who is very beautiful
   B. Amnon feigns illness and says he can only be fed by Tamar
   C. Amnon brutally rapes Tamar and then rejects her
   D. Other brother, Absalom, takes Tamar into his home and seeks revenge on Amnon
   E. At gathering of all brothers, Absalom has Amnon killed, and other brothers scatter

III. ABSALOM REBELS AGAINST DAVID
   A. Absalom calls together his allies at Hebron
   B. David hears of rebellion, yet does not fight
   C. David abandons Jerusalem to avoid being overtaken by Absalom
   D. Absalom takes over Jerusalem and civil war begins
      1. Absalom humiliates David by lying with concubines in daylight, then pursues David
      2. In battle between father's and son's armies, Absalom's hair is caught in branches of tree and he "hangs between heaven and earth"
      3. David's men find Absalom and kill him
      4. David mourns his lost son: "Absalom, my son! If only I had died instead of you."

IV. FORESHADOWING OF JESUS
   A. Jesus travels same path as David when he leaves Jerusalem
   B. "Father forgive them. They know not what they are doing."
   C. Jesus dies in place of his children

DAVID THE KING

LESSON SIX

ABSALOM, MY SON!

In the sixth and final talk, Bishop Barron introduces us to some of the events in David's life that take place after his kingdom is established: his sin with Bathsheba, and events surrounding his children Tamar, Amnon, and Absalom.

A TURNING POINT

Immediately after the establishment of the Davidic Covenant, David does two things that show the radical faithfulness with which he entered into that relationship with the Lord:

First, David shows his love for God above all things, with his whole heart, his whole soul, and all his might (Deut 6:4), by subduing foreign peoples in the land of Israel. We saw previously that this was a task close to David's heart. He was taking care of Saul's unfinished business with the Amalekites, and he was the first person in all Israel to overcome the Jebusites and so conquer Jerusalem. Yet even the conquering of Jerusalem was closer to the beginning than the end of the unfinished business that remained after the period of the Judges. There were a number of foreign peoples still to be subdued among the Israelites. Accordingly, David set about "doing battle with evil all the way down," and was so successful that we are told in only a few short verses that he nearly completed the job (2 Sam 8:1-14).

Second, David shows us how he loves his neighbor as himself (Lev 19:18). For the sake of Saul's son, Jonathan, David seeks out a member of the house of Saul to whom he can show kindness (2 Sam 9:1). He finds Mephibosheth, a grandson of Jonathan, who is lame in both feet (2 Sam 9:13). Out of purely gratuitous love David lavishes him with the entire wealth of Saul's house, and grants him the privilege of always eating at David's table (2 Sam 9:9-10). Mephibosheth thereby becomes like an adopted son of David.

DAVID THE KING

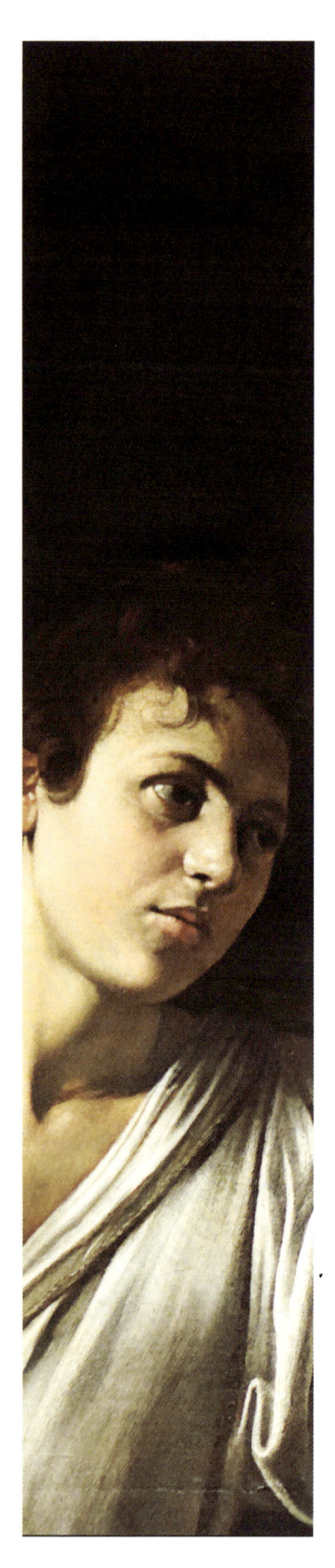

At this point, we reach a turning point in David's life to which Bishop Barron referred in Talk 3. In the spring, " the time when kings go to war, David sent out Joab along with his officers and all Israel, and they laid waste the Ammonites and besieged Rabbah. *David himself remained in Jerusalem*" (2 Sam 11:1, emphasis added). In the days when troops wore only natural fibers and moved either on foot or in open-air chariots, the difficulties that cold weather presented made it simply impractical to bring an army out to war in the winter. Whatever a king's aspirations or grievances might have been, he had to put his military pursuits on hold until the spring thaw made the mobility of the army possible again. Consequently, the spring was a very busy time for a "man of valor, a man of war" (1 Sam 16:18) such as King David. It was the time when he could finally march out and begin setting things to rights (militarily speaking, that is).

It is not clear why David stayed home this particular year. Perhaps David felt as though his previous year's conquests were enough and that he had successfully fulfilled the will of the Lord for the people of Israel. But if that is so David was utterly mistaken. He thinks that he has done battle with evil "all the way down," but his actions evoke those of Adam in the garden. As Bishop Barron pointed out in Talk 2, the very presence of the serpent in the Garden bears witness to a similar laziness on Adam's part in his duty to till and protect it. All it took was that one serpent to tempt Adam into letting the entirety of paradise come crashing to a halt. So it was to be also with David.

It was "late one afternoon, when David arose from his couch" (2 Sam 11:2). This should remind us of Adam and Eve, walking "in the cool of the day" after their own sin (Gen. 3:8). The fact that David is just getting up from his couch so late should also remind us of Adam's laziness in the garden. Upon arising from his nap, David takes a walk upon the roof of the palace and sees a beautiful woman bathing (2 Sam 11:2). Her beauty, like that of Saul and of David himself, spells trouble.

David inquires after her and learns that she is the wife of Uriah, one of the soldiers of his army (2 Sam 11:3). Thereupon "David sent messengers" (note that he sends multiple men) "and took her" (note the implication of the use of force), "and she came to him, and he lay with her" (2 Sam 11:4). David thus violates the sixth commandment, a capital offense under the Mosaic Law (Lev 20:10). Bathsheba, by contrast, remains faithful to the Law. Even though David compels her to lay with him, she still observes the Law for ritual bathing following intercourse, before she returns home (Lev 15:18; 2 Sam 11:4-5).

As a result of the adultery, Bathsheba conceives a child (2 Sam 11:5). Instead of admitting his guilt, David contrives a plan to cover up his sin. He will invite Uriah home from battle, hoping that Uriah will lie with his wife and so mistakenly think that the child is his own. Putting aside the fact that "the Lord sees the heart," the cover-up is doomed to fail for two reasons. First, it would fail because in the ancient world there were no pregnancy tests; Bathsheba would not have known that she was pregnant until she skipped at least one menstrual cycle, and so by the time Uriah arrived home from battle it would have been almost too late for David to claim that the child was Uriah's. Secondly and more importantly, David does not account for Uriah's faithfulness to David's military discipline.

Let us recall from 1 Samuel that when David and his companions were hungry and they encountered Ahimelech the priest, David said to Ahimelech:

> "Now what do you have on hand? Give me five loaves, or whatever you can find." But the priest replied to David, "I have no ordinary bread on hand, only holy bread; if the men have abstained from women, you may eat some of that." David answered the priest: "*We have indeed stayed away from women. In the past whenever I went out on a campaign, all the young men were consecrated—even for an ordinary campaign.*" (1 Sam 21:4-6; emphasis added)

David, having abandoned his former discipline, tries to incite Uriah to do the same. But Uriah is so faithful to David's former discipline that he swears an oath not to violate it in even stronger terms than David had originally spoken to Ahimelech.

> Uriah answered David, "The ark and Israel and Judah are staying in tents, and my lord Joab and my lord's servants are encamped in the open field. Can I go home to eat and to drink and to sleep with my wife? As the LORD lives and as you live, I will do no such thing." (2 Sam 11:11)

So David goes with Plan B. David instructs Joab, the commander of the army, to send Uriah to the front lines and then to withdraw from him so that Uriah is struck down (2 Sam 11:15). In a special act of cruelty, he sends the letter "by the hand of Uriah" (2 Sam 11:14). Joab complies and Uriah is struck down (2 Sam 11:16-18). David thereby violates the fifth commandment by the willful murder of Uriah, another capital offense under the Law (Exod 21:12).

DAVID THE KING

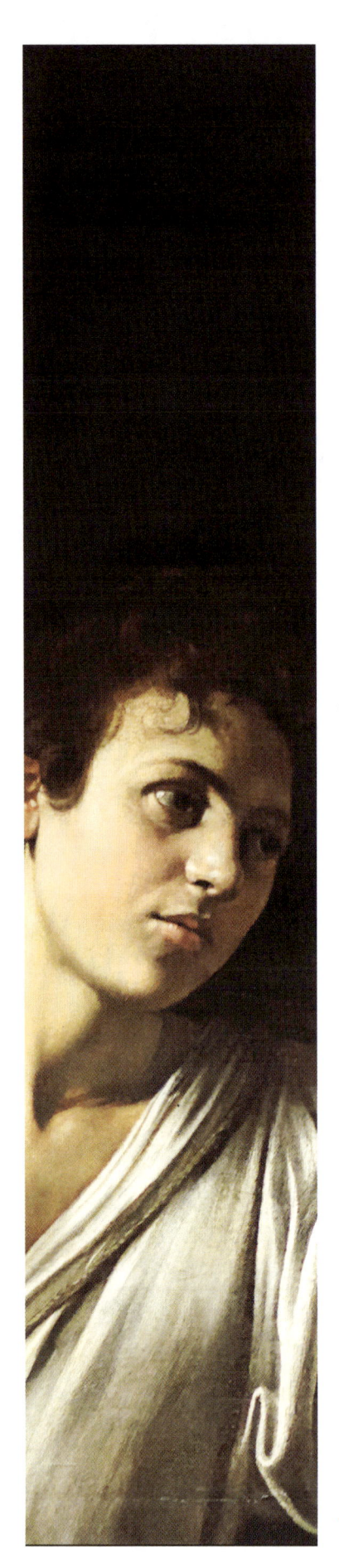

Finally, with Uriah dead, David achieves his aim. When the period of mourning was over, "David sent and brought her to his house, and she became his wife" (2 Sam 11:27). If David could not pass the child off as Uriah's, he would feign the child's legitimacy by murdering Uriah and marrying his wife.

The prophet Nathan, who only a few chapters ago had spoken the words of the Davidic Covenant to David, is now given the unenviable task of having to convict David of these two grievous sins. Under prophetic inspiration, he comes up with a plan: he will tell David a parable in which a rich man steals a poor man's lamb, and so get David—as king over Israel—to pronounce judgment over himself. The plan works. David pronounces his own judgment: "As the Lord lives, the man who has done this deserves to die; and he shall restore the lamb fourfold, because he did this thing, and because he had no pity" (2 Sam 12:5-6).

At that point, Nathan responds to David with chilling words: "You are the man" (2 Sam 12:5-6). He then pronounces the divine judgment. The judgment has two parts. One part is the fourfold restitution (2 Sam 12:10-14):

1. "The sword shall never depart from your house…"
2. "I will raise up evil against you out of your own house…"
3. "I will take your wives before your eyes…"
4. "And [I will] give them to your neighbor… and [your neighbor] shall lie with your wives in the sight of this sun."

There is another part that Nathan does not speak. It is the same punishment that was given to Eli for his abuse of the priestly office. David had committed two capital offenses and he had pronounced his own death sentence. David knows what is coming next.

Rather than waiting around for Nathan to finish the Lord's judgment, he interrupts the prophet with a sincere and contrite confession. "I have sinned against the Lord" (2 Sam 12:13). We can judge the sincerity of the confession from the Lord's response. The Lord forgives him and permits him to live. The child's life, however, is not spared. Since the child conceived by the adultery could have been David's heir, and since the Lord does not use sin as a direct means of fulfilling his promises, David's actions placed his child in an impossible situation and so sealed the child's early fate (2 Sam 12:14).

THE AFTERMATH

As a personal, royal, and priestly failure, the sin with Bathsheba fundamentally alters David's life. It is a personal failure because he rejected the Lord through mortal sin. It is a royal failure because he committed his sins by failing in discipline (by not going out with his men), abusing his power (by lounging while his men were fighting), abusing his servants (whom he sent to get Bathsheba), abusing Bathsheba, and abusing his authority (by sending Uriah to die). It is a priestly failure because he showed utter contempt for the Law, even while Bathsheba painstakingly observed it.

As a result, David appears as a recapitulation of Eli: a failed leader and priest, who abuses his office, oppresses the poor, encourages sexual sin, and who—we are going to find out—is lax with his rebellious sons. From that point forward David will grow increasingly like Eli as he approaches more and more the figure of the "inactive king." First, when the Israelites are on the verge of victory against the Ammonites, he has to be called out to the field so that it will at least appear that he had something to do with the victory (2 Sam 12:28). Later, as Bishop Barron explains, he will flee Jerusalem rather than battle for its control (2 Sam 15:14). By the end of the book, David is completely sapped of his former vigor. The man who slew Goliath and vanquished the enemies of Israel grows so "weary" that in another fight against the Philistines "David's men adjured him, 'You shall no more go out with us to battle, lest you quench the lamp of Israel'" (2 Sam 21:17).

Between the first and the last of these battles, David receives the fourfold punishment promised by Nathan.

"The sword shall never depart from your house..."

The first punishment is related to the first promise that God made to David in the Davidic Covenant. The promise, as we heard in Talk 5, was to give David "rest from all his enemies round about." It represented the gift of rest that only radical fidelity to the Lord could merit, and which David alone among the leaders of Israel had brought to the people.

Since David has now broken that fidelity, David is going to lose something of that rest. He will not lose what God promised him in a strict sense. As we heard in Talk 5, the Davidic Covenant was something that God swore an oath never to break. Since God promised "rest from all his enemies round about," David will not be seriously threatened by any foreign powers. Instead,

God decrees that David shall suffer from a different kind of turmoil: internal turmoil. Rather than being plagued by the swords of foreign powers, or even of foreigners within the land of Israel, David will be plagued by violent unrest within his own household.

As Bishop Barron recounts, the trouble begins when one of David's sons, Amnon, rapes his half-sister, Tamar (2 Sam 13:1-20). It is a terrible crime, which will mean the ruining of Tamar's earthly life henceforth. David hears of the deed, and "he was very angry" (2 Sam 13:21), but he does nothing, even though the Mosaic Law charged that any man who lay with his half-sister be cut off from the people (Lev 18:9, 29; Lev 20:17) and cursed (Deut 27:22). Even Eli chastised his sons; we are not told that David even took that small step of correction.

Understandably, Tamar's full-brother, Absalom, is angry; but his anger turns to hatred (2 Sam 13:22). He avenges the wrong done to Tamar by murdering Amnon (2 Sam 13:23-29), inflicting vigilante vengeance upon him that went a step beyond the punishment stipulated by the Law. Aware that murder is a capital offense under the Law (Exod 21:12, 14; Lev 24:17; Num 35:16-21), he flees for sanctuary to his maternal grandfather outside of Israel for three years (2 Sam 3:3; 2 Sam 13:37).

After three years, David is tricked into inviting him back. The incident is a parody of Nathan's condemnation. Nathan was a prophet, serving justice on behalf of the Lord. He used a parable to get David to pronounce a just sentence in accordance with the Law. David's commander, Joab, convinces a woman to tell David a parable that gets him to do the opposite. Instead of giving Absalom the punishment he deserves, the woman convinces David to ignore the Law altogether and invite Absalom back (2 Sam 14:1-24).

"I will raise up evil against you out of your own house..."

Up until this point, Absalom seems like an otherwise just man who got carried away with anger in a horrible situation. However, as Bishop Barron points out, the Deuteronomistic Historian gives us a telling detail about Absalom that suggests worse things to come:

©2017 Word on Fire Catholic Ministries

> In all Israel there was no man more praised for his beauty than Absalom, flawless from the sole of his foot to the crown of his head. When he shaved his head—as he used to do at the end of every year, because his hair became too heavy for him—the hair weighed two hundred shekels [about 5 lbs] according to the royal standard. (2 Sam 14:25-26)

Let us recall with Bishop Barron that these indications of beauty always foreshadowed trouble. It is no different with Absalom. After two years on probation (2 Sam 14:24, 28), he decides boldly to appear before David, effectively flaunting his guilt, saying to Joab, "if there is guilt in me, let him kill me" (2 Sam 14:32). Of course, there *is* guilt in Absalom. But Absalom is confident that David will do nothing about it, and Absalom is right (2 Sam 14:33).

Once Absalom confirms that he can walk around David's kingdom with impunity for the murder of Amnon, he attempts a full-scale *coup d'état*. As Bishop Barron describes, he gets himself a band of followers (2 Sam 15:1), and begins to woo the hearts of the people (2 Sam 15:2-6). Then Absalom plays a trick on David: he convinces David to allow him to go to Hebron under the false pretense of fulfilling a vow to worship the Lord, and while there he carries out a double usurpation: assuming to himself David's kingly and priestly offices (2 Sam 15:10-12). He thus attempts to fashion himself as a complete replacement for David, beginning from the place where David originally assumed the kingship over Judah.

"I will take your wives before your eyes..."

With the rebellion of Absalom, the great house of David begins to crumble, and David effectively abdicates his role as *paterfamilias*. Sensing the strength of Absalom's support, David observes that "the hearts of the men of Israel have gone after Absalom" (2 Sam 15:13). So, as Bishop Barron describes, he decides to leave Jerusalem—that nearly impregnable city—and flee (2 Sam 15:14).

The retreat from Jerusalem, as Bishop Barron also notes, is a reversal of the triumphal procession undertaken when David entered the city with the Ark. David and his followers proceed down through the Kidron Valley to the Mount of Olives, retracing the steps taken to come into the city originally, the joy of their entry having been turned into the sorrow of their exit:

> As David went up the ascent of the Mount of Olives, he wept without ceasing. His head was covered, and he was walking barefoot. All those who were with him also had their heads covered and were weeping as they went. (2 Sam 15:30)

DAVID THE KING

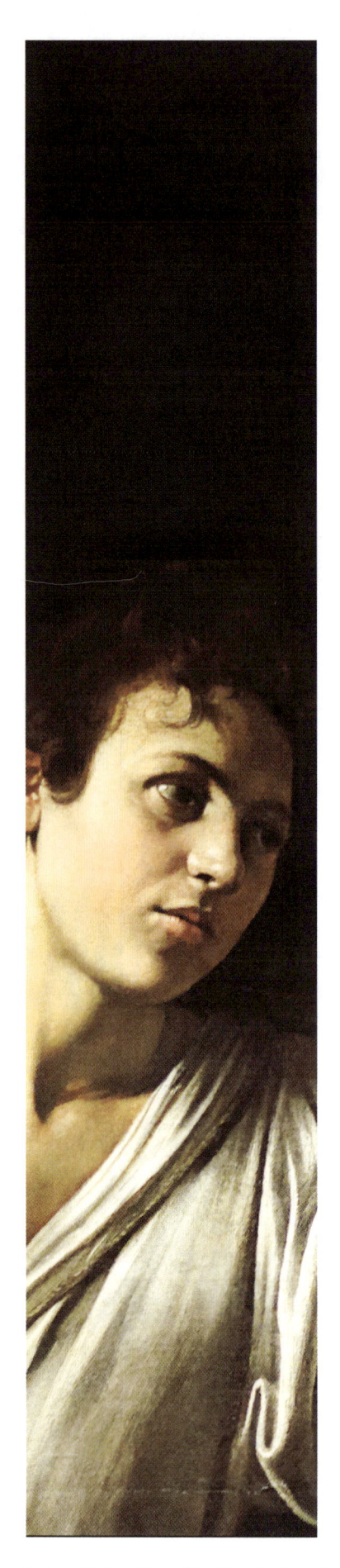

As David flees, we are given a curious detail about his arrangements: "So the king went forth, and all his household after him. And the king left ten concubines to keep the house" (2 Sam 15:15). When David was faithful to the Lord, he was given the city, a great house within the city, and large family within that house as a sign of the Lord's blessing. Now that by his sin he has lost the Lord's blessing, the city is torn from him, as is the house, as are ten of his wives who live in it, just as the Lord spoke by Nathan.

"And [I will] give them to your neighbor... and [your neighbor] shall lie with your wives in the sight of this sun."

Then David's sin comes full circle. After David flees Jerusalem, Absalom enters the city and takes counsel about what he should do to solidify his grip over Israel. Ahithophel, his counselor, advises him to lie with the ten wives whom David left to watch over the royal household, as a sign of dominance over David (2 Sam 16:20-21). So they put a tent upon the roof of David's house, the very place from which David originally gazed upon Bathsheba and from which he sent for her (2 Sam 11:2), and Absalom lies with David's wives in view of everyone. Thus the place from which David first sinned against marriage becomes the place where Absalom sins against David's marriages. David's household is destroyed, and Absalom adds incest, another capital crime, to murder (Lev 20:11).

ABSALOM, THE BETRAYER

Allegorically, Absalom is a figure of Judas, who, as a disciple of Jesus, is set to inherit an apostleship, and yet who attempts to rebel against Jesus and betray him into the hands of the Romans. While Judas' vice was avarice instead of vanity, his vice had the similar effect of being the cause of his own undoing, as he betrays the Savior for a mere thirty pieces of silver.

Tropologically, Absalom warns us that no matter how close we come to Jesus, how faithfully we may serve him, or how much authority may be entrusted to our care, there will always be temptations to rebellion. These temptations, like the rebellions of Satan, of Judas, and of others in the history of Israel and of the Church, always promise

> more than they can deliver. Jesus, the Son of David, has been eternally victorious over sin and death (1 Cor 15:54-56), and so the promise made to the son of David has been fulfilled: "your house and your kingdom shall be made sure for ever before me; your throne shall be established forever" (2 Sam 7:16). There is nothing we can do to dislodge Jesus from his throne, but "if we endure, we shall also reign with him" (2 Tim 2:12).

†

RECLAIMING JERUSALEM

In the midst of all this, Bishop Barron points us to the importance of a man named Shime-i. Shime-i is from the house of Saul, a house which was still grieving over the loss of the kingship (2 Sam 16:8). Shime-i ridicules David and sees in Absalom's usurpation a just reward for the replacement of Saul by David. While Shime-i was certainly incorrect to make any association between David's and Absalom's respective accessions to the throne of Israel, it is noteworthy that David refuses to correct him. In fact, David even refuses his servant's request to stop the man from ridiculing him.

David's words to Shime-i point us to the fundamental difference between David, on the one hand, and Eli and Saul, on the other. They show us that David has accepted the gravity of his sin and the justice of his humiliation, and his words show us the depth of David's contrition.

> Suppose the LORD has told him to curse David; who then will dare to say, "Why are you doing this?" Then David said to Abishai and to all his servants: "If my own son, who came forth from my loins, is seeking my life, how much more might this Benjaminite do so! Let him alone and let him curse, for the LORD has told him to. Perhaps the LORD will look upon my affliction and repay me with good for the curses he is uttering this day." (2 Sam 16:10-12)

David sees Shime-i's insults as a divinely appointed penance; David accepts the penance, and offers it up for deliverance from his sin. One senses that David's acceptance of Shime-i represents his acceptance of all the divinely appointed consequences of his actions.

This acceptance, together with the contrition that accompanies it, begins to redeem David's situation. It marks the beginning of his return as king, and the beginning of victory.

If David is to return as king, that is not to say that he will return as king in all his former glory. He musters his army for battle, but obeys his men's entreaty for him to stay behind "at the side of the gate" (2 Sam 18:1-4). Bishop Barron recalls here the image of Eli, fattened on his feasts, unable to fight, waiting with bated breath for news of the battle. The result for David will be no different than the result for Eli. Absalom is killed, caught in a tree by his vainly tended hair, and struck down against David's orders by Joab (2 Sam 18:9-15).

Even if David looked a lot like Eli in his sin and now as he waits and hears news of his son's death in battle, David's attitude of penance leads to an entirely different reaction to the bad news than that of Eli. When news of the deaths of Phinehas and Hophni was brought to Eli, Eli was so shocked that such a thing could happen to him that he fell over backwards and died. Even though Samuel had prophesied those deaths to Eli, we see in the shock of Eli the failure to accept the consequences of his actions. By contrast, when news is brought to David of Absalom's death, David evinces no shock. As Bishop Barron describes, he is fully aware that this situation is his own fault, that the death of his son is one possible consequence, and he has already accepted with contrition the consequences of his sins, offering them up to the Lord in expiation for his sins. When he receives the terrible news of his son's death, he responds not with shock but with sorrow. In lines that are as deeply human as they are sanctified by penitent grief, we hear David's lament, "O my son Absalom, my son, my son Absalom! If only I had died instead of you, O Absalom, my son, my son!" (2 Sam 19:1).

The return of David to the kingship mirrors his original ascent. It begins with his own tribe, the tribe of Judah. Building upon the natural relationship among his kinsmen, David slowly rallies them to himself and rebuilds that "mystical body of David."

As when David first became king, rallying his own tribe to him was a much easier task than rallying the rest of the country. When he first became king, the northern tribes went after Ish-bosheth, and it was only after

Ish-bosheth's assassination that David was able to exercise kingship over all Israel. Now the northern tribes follow a man named Sheba (2 Sam 20:1-2). He, like Ish-bosheth, is a short-lived leader. The army of David pursues him into a city, and rather than face a siege or an assault, the inhabitants of the city deliver him up to Joab (2 Sam 20:14-22). Unlike when David first became king and he was leading the army himself, now that David is at the end of his military career he decides to assume the throne of his kingdom while his army is still out chasing Sheba.

Through David's contrition, his resignation to the will of God, his penitential spirit, and the expiatory power of his sufferings, David returns to faithfulness in the Lord and so is restored to many of the blessings he previously enjoyed. God redeems David's sin, and Solomon, the first legitimate son born to David and Bathsheba, succeeds David as king over Israel.

†

THE SPIRITUAL SENSES

In the previous two talks, as we saw David rise from the position of a shepherd boy to a great king of Israel, it was easier to see how David, in the allegorical sense, was a figure of Christ. In the events discussed in this lesson, it is understandably a bit more difficult. Christ, after all, "knew no sin" (2 Cor 5:21). David, meanwhile, caused many of these events by committing multiple mortal sins.

The key to David's allegorical significance is easier to see if we first consider his tropological significance. For even more clearly than David is a figure of *Christ*, David is revealed to us in the latter part of Second Samuel as the figure of each *Christian*.

By virtue of original sin, all humans have a participation in the sin of Adam, as well as in his exclusion from paradise (CCC 402). We are all, consequently, in need of supernatural grace to purge and heal us from sin, as well as to elevate us into supernatural friendship with God (CCC 1997-1999). Our need for grace, while rooted in original sin, is made all the more urgent by personal sin, which more deeply injures ourselves, our communities, and our relationships with God (CCC 1849).

The "good news" of the Gospel is not just that Jesus took upon himself the punishment due our sins, but that he went before us and offered to God the love that we withheld, thereby giving to us the means of our redemption (CCC 606-607). When we are incorporated into that redemption through the Sacrament of Baptism, and reincorporated into it by the

DAVID THE KING

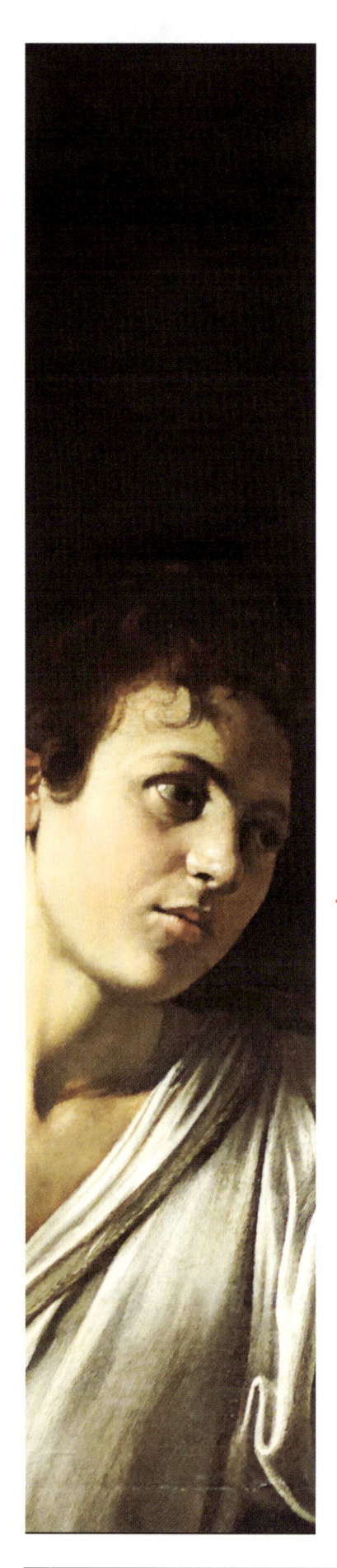

Sacrament of Penance, we are enabled to "take part in Christ's Passion" because we are cleansed from our sins (CCC 1987-1988). Moreover, when the grace of Christ enables us to share in Christ's Passion, a paradoxical mystery takes place: we are empowered to share in the expiation of our own sins, and even those of others. That power is rooted primarily in the action of Jesus, but in virtue of the forgiveness that Jesus imparts to us through the Sacraments, our participation in that action is real, just like the human authorship of Scripture is real (CCC 1459-1460).

Ignatius of Antioch fully understood the importance of this paradox. As he was being led to martyrdom, he prayed that he—though already a bishop—would be strengthened for martyrdom so that he could be a "true Christian." How is it that he did not think he was already a Christian? The answer is that while he was already a Christian in name, he did not think that his life would really *look like Christ's* in actual fact until he had "laid down his life for his friends" as Christ did.

It is in that sense that David appears in the latter part of Second Samuel as a figure of Christ. David is not sinless by any means; the Deuteronomistic Historian recounts his sins and all their consequences in painstaking detail. But David is a figure of Christ precisely insofar as, by repenting from his sins with true contrition, bearing the consequences with true love, and so offering up those consequences with true Christian forbearance, he made full and complete expiation and satisfaction for his past life. That is why, when the consequences get to their most painful points, after David has undone his triumphal entry into Jerusalem by marching in the mournful dirge to the Mount of Olives, and as he weeps over his dead son who had betrayed him, Bishop Barron can rightfully point out that David remains for us a powerful figure of Jesus weeping over Jerusalem and forgiving his enemies. It may have been easier to see how David fulfilled the two greatest commandments before his sins with Bathsheba and Uriah. But, if we know how to read this text with the analogy of faith, the Christological greatness of David appears even more powerfully in his penance for those sins afterwards. With that, we can see even more deeply why the inspired authors of the New Testament looked to David as the hinge around which the entire Old Testament revolved. David was for them, as he is for us, a man after God's own heart—in his simple origins, in his meteoric rise, in his faithful rule and prayer, and finally in his humble and heartfelt repentance.

QUESTIONS FOR UNDERSTANDING

1. What are the two greatest commandments, and how does David honor them before the incident with Bathsheba? (Deut 6:4-5; Matt 22:36-40; 1 Kings 15:5; 2 Sam 9:1-10)

2. How does David's sin with Bathsheba mirror Adam's sin in the Garden of Eden? (2 Sam 11:1-17; Gen 3:1-7; CCC 397-398)

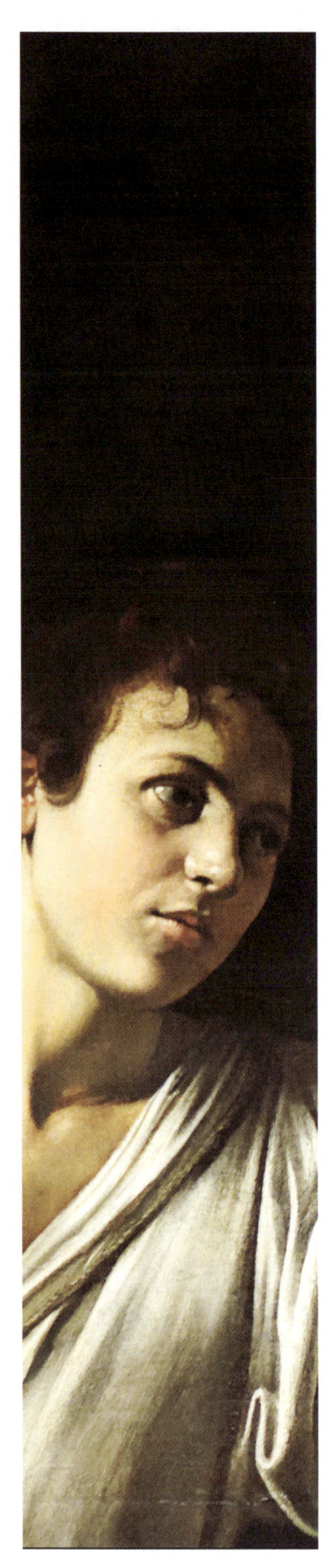

3. What are the four consequences that Nathan promises to David? How are they fulfilled in David's subsequent interactions with his children? (2 Sam 12:9-12; 13; 14:33; 15:10-12, 13-16; 16:20-22)

4. What spiritual quality allows David to retake Jerusalem and the kingdom? (2 Sam 16:5-12; 2 Sam 18:31-32; 19:1; CCC 1450)

QUESTIONS FOR APPLICATION

1. What can you do to promote the virtues of chastity and purity in your family and community?

2. What are the consequences of an "inactive king"? How can you guard against inactivity in your own life in those matters where others are entrusted to your care?

3. What can the story of David teach us about the nature and importance of family?

4. How can David's penitential attitude help you better understand what it means to be a figure of Christ in your own life?

BIOGRAPHICAL INFORMATION

MOST REVEREND ROBERT E. BARRON

Bishop Robert Barron is an acclaimed author, speaker, and theologian. He is also the founder of the global media ministry *Word on Fire*, which reaches millions of people by utilizing the tools of new media to draw people into or back to the Catholic Faith. Francis Cardinal George has described him as "one of the Church's best messengers."

Bishop Barron is the creator and host of CATHOLICISM (2011), a groundbreaking, award-winning documentary series about the Catholic Faith. The series has aired on hundreds of PBS stations across the world and has been used by parishes, universities, and schools as an essential resource. Since then, Bishop Barron and Word on Fire also released the follow-up documentary CATHOLICISM: *The New Evangelization* (2013) and are currently wrapping up CATHOLICISM: *The Pivotal Players*, a beautiful new film series on the mystics, scholars, artists, and saints who shaped the Church and changed the world. The series debuted in September 2016 and has been syndicated for national television.

Bishop Barron's website, *WordOnFire.org*, reaches millions of people each year. The site hosts daily blog posts, weekly articles and video commentaries, and an extensive audio archive of over 500 homilies. In addition, Bishop Barron also sends out daily email reflections on the Gospel to hundreds of thousands of readers, and episodes of his podcast, *The Word on Fire Show*, have been downloaded over two million times.

EWTN (The Eternal Word Television Network) and CatholicTV broadcast Bishop Barron's videos and documentaries to a worldwide audience of over 150 million people. His weekly homilies and podcasts air on multiple radio stations to millions of listeners.

Bishop Barron works with NBC News in New York as an on-air contributor and analyst. He is also a frequent commentator for the *Chicago Tribune*, FOX News, CNN, EWTN, Our Sunday Visitor, the *Catholic Herald* in London, and Catholic News Agency.

He has published numerous essays and articles on theology and the spiritual life, which appear frequently online and in numerous journals. He is a #1 Amazon bestselling author and has published thirteen books.

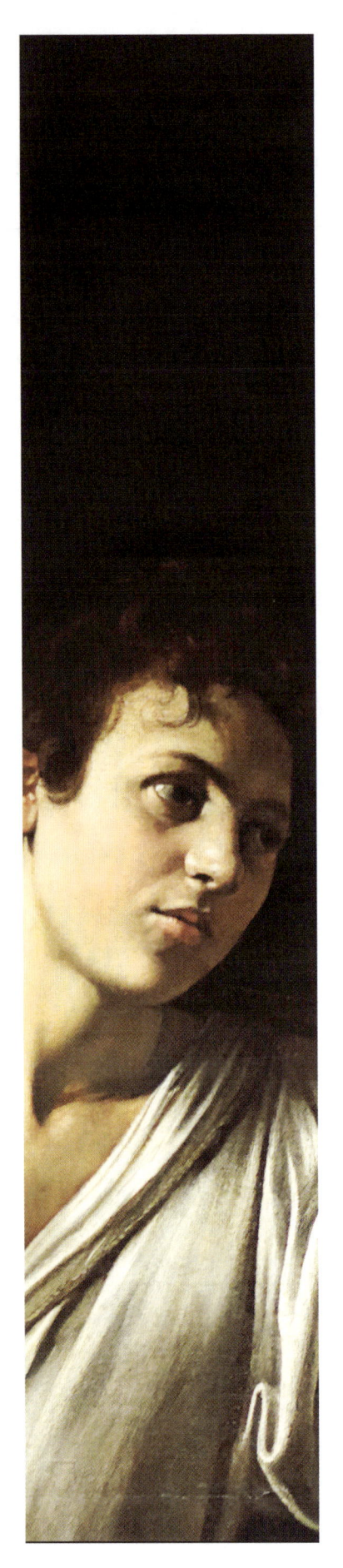

On July 21, 2015, Pope Francis appointed Bishop Barron to be Auxiliary Bishop of the Archdiocese of Los Angeles. He was ordained bishop on September 8, 2015. He previously served as the Rector/President of Mundelein Seminary University of St. Mary of the Lake from 2012 until 2015. He was appointed to the theological faculty of Mundelein Seminary in 1992, and has also served as a visiting professor at the University of Notre Dame and at the Pontifical University of St. Thomas Aquinas. He was twice scholar in residence at the Pontifical North American College at the Vatican.

Ordained in 1986 in the Archdiocese of Chicago, Bishop Barron received a Master's Degree in Philosophy from the Catholic University of America in 1982 and a doctorate in Sacred Theology from the Institut Catholique de Paris in 1992.

DR. JACOB WOOD

Though originally from New Jersey, Dr. Jacob W. Wood received a Masters of Theology (Honours) from the University of St. Andrews, Scotland, in 2007. The love for the Scriptures and the Christian Tradition which he developed there led him to the doorstep of the Catholic Church, into which he was received in 2008.

Following his conversion, Dr. Wood continued his theological studies at the Catholic University of America, where in 2014 he received a Ph.D. in Systematic Theology. He has taught theology at Catholic institutions of higher learning across the United States, and is presently an Assistant Professor of Theology at Franciscan University of Steubenville.

In addition to his teaching, Dr. Wood is the author of *Speaking the Love of God: An Introduction to the Sacraments* (Emmaus Road, 2016). He has also published scholarly articles in *Nova et Vetera* and *The Heythrop Journal*, as well as popular articles in *National Review Online*, *Inside the Vatican Magazine*, *Crisis Magazine*, and *Aleteia*. He lives in Bloomingdale, OH, with his wife and four children, where together they enjoy gardening and raising animals amidst the beauty of the Ohio countryside.

GLOSSARY

AARONIDE PRIEST: A male patrilineal descendent of Moses' brother, Aaron, consecrated to the priesthood in order to offer sacrifice.

AIKIDO: A martial art in which the principal means of self-defense is the use of an opponent's momentum against him.

ALLEGORICAL SENSE: The spiritual sense of Scripture that considers how the literal sense of a passage in the Old Testament refers to Christ and his Church.

ANAGOGICAL SENSE: The spiritual sense of Scripture that considers how the literal sense of a passage in the Old Testament refers to the union of God with the soul both now and in eternity.

ARK OF THE COVENANT: The gilded box which God commanded the Israelites to make at the Sinai Covenant, and which housed the tablets of the Law, Aaron's staff, and a piece of manna from the wilderness. There was a mercy seat on top of the ark, which represented God's throne and his presence among the people of Israel.

BABYLONIAN CAPTIVITY: The period from 586 BC to 538 BC, which the inhabitants of the Kingdom of Judah spent in forced exile throughout the Babylonian Empire.

CEREAL OFFERING: An offering of flour, oil, and salt stipulated by the Mosaic Law.

CUBIT: An ancient unit of measurement taken as the distance from the elbow to the tip of the middle finger, generally reckoned as about eighteen inches.

DAVIDIC COVENANT: The relationship established by God with Israel through David in 2 Sam 7, and the promises made by God to David in that context: rest from David's enemies round about, and a perpetual Davidic dynastic line.

DEUTERONOMIC COVENANT: The name given by scholars to the covenant between God and Israel in the Book of Deuteronomy. Some scholars believe this covenant to be distinct from the Sinai Covenant, and to amend the Sinai Covenant in light of the Golden Calf incident.

DEUTERONOMIST: The inspired author(s) whom Julius Wellhausen hypothesized to have written the Book of Deuteronomy.

DEUTERONOMISTIC HISTORIAN: The inspired author(s) whom scholars believe to have written the Deuteronomistic History.

DEUTERONOMISTIC HISTORY: The name given by scholars to the narrative that tells the story of Israel's conquest of Canaan, its development from a federation of tribes into a kingdom, and the initial dissolution of that kingdom at the time of the Babylonian Captivity. In the Bible, it runs from the Book of Joshua through the Book of 2 Kings.

EPHOD: A linen garment associated specifically with the priesthood under the Mosaic Law. David uses the ephod as a sacramental prior to the conquest of Jerusalem, and puts on the ephod once he assumes the office of priest-king according to the order of Melchizedek.

GRATIA PRIMA: The Catholic principle that all of our meritorious actions begin with grace and continue under human cooperation.

GRATIA SOLA: The Protestant principle that we do not perform meritorious actions because, while our actions begin with grace, they do not continue under human cooperation.

GUILT OFFERING: An offering of a male sheep stipulated by the Mosaic Law in reparation for an unwitting sin, or for any other sin, stipulated in Lev 6:1-7.

HIGH PRIEST: The leader of all the Aaronide priests and the Levites, and the direct patrilineal descendant of Moses' brother Aaron. Until the reign of Solomon, the high priest could be descended from Aaron either through Eleazar or through Ithamar. During the reign of David, there were two high priests, one descended from Eleazar and one descended through Ithamar. Subsequently, Solomon deposed the successor of Ithamar as a punishment for rebellion, and high priests were afterwards drawn exclusively from the house of Eleazar.

HOLY OF HOLIES: The innermost part of the Tabernacle, and later the innermost part of the Temple, in which the Ark of the Covenant was housed.

INSPIRATION: The charism given to the human authors of Sacred Scripture whereby the words they chose as human authors would also be the words that God chose as the divine author.

ISRAEL: The name of God's chosen people in the Old Testament, taken from the name given to the patriarch Jacob after his struggle with the angel. After the split of the united kingdom in the tenth century BC, it was also the name of the Northern Kingdom, which encompassed ten of the twelve tribes.

JUDAH: The tribe from which David and Jesus Christ were born. After the split of the United Kingdom in the tenth century BC, it was also the name of the Southern Kingdom, which encompassed the tribes of Judah and Benjamin.

JUDGE: The leader of Israel from the time of Joshua until the anointing of Saul as king. The judicial office was a non-hereditary office, appointed by God periodically to deliver the people of Israel from their foreign enemies and restore them to the blessings of peace.

LEVIRITE MARRIAGE: A marriage between a man and his deceased brother's widow, required by the Mosaic Law to provide a name and an inheritance for the deceased.

LEVITE: After the Golden Calf incident, a consecrated man of the tribe of Levi but not among Aaron's descendants. The Levites assisted the Aaronide priests with the duties of the Tabernacle, and later the Temple.

LITERAL SENSE: The principal meaning of a given passage of Scripture intended by the human and divine authors of that passage. It is not a "plain sense," nor is it necessarily a historical sense, depending on the genre of the passage.

MASHIACH (MESSIAH): The Hebrew title for the "anointed one" of God, whom the people of Israel believed would be sent to redeem the people of God and gather them into the Kingdom of God. The Greek word for *Mashiach* is *Christos*, which is rendered in English as "Christ." In the Old Testament, prophets, priests, and kings could be anointed, and so the *Mashiach* has a threefold prophetic, priestly, and royal office.

MOSAIC LAW: The Law given by God through Moses to the Israelites at Mt. Sinai.

NAZIRITE: A person dedicated to the Lord for a certain period of time, during which he or she abstained from alcohol and from cutting his or her hair; Nazirites observed the same ascetical disciplines as priests and Levites would when going into the Temple to offer sacrifice.

NECROMANCY: Conjuration of the spirits of the dead for purposes of magically revealing the future or influencing the course of events.

PATERFAMILIAS: The male head of an ancient household, who possessed legal authority over all the people and goods in the household.

PEACE OFFERING: An offering of an animal stipulated by the Mosaic Law. It was the only offering among the major non-holiday offerings in which the people were also afforded a share of the meat of the sacrificial animal. Peace offerings were subdivided into thanksgiving offerings, to which was added an offering of cakes, and votive offerings.

PENTATEUCH: The first five books of the Bible: Genesis, Exodus, Leviticus, Numbers, and Deuteronomy. In Hebrew, it is called the *Torah*.

PROVIDENCE: The action by which God directs all created things towards their ultimate fulfillment in him.

RULE OF CHARITY: The rule of biblical interpretation that suggests that we should interpret any given passage of Scripture in a way that builds up the love of God and the love of neighbor, because all Scripture is inspired by the Holy Spirit, and the Holy Spirit's purpose in all things is to increase those two loves.

RULE OF FAITH: The rule of biblical interpretation that suggests that we should interpret any given passage of Scripture according to the faith of the Church, because all Scripture is inspired by the Holy Spirit, and it is that same Holy Spirit that guides the Church into all truth.

RULE OF THE FATHERS: The rule of biblical interpretation that suggests that we should never interpret Scripture contrary to the unanimous consent of the Church Fathers, because the Fathers are among the primary vehicles through whom the Tradition of the Faith has been passed down to subsequent generations.

SHEKEL: An ancient unit of weight. It is the equivalent of approximately eleven to seventeen grams.

SIN OFFERING: An offering of an animal stipulated by the Mosaic Law. The particular animal offered depended upon who committed the sin: a priest, a ruler, a common person, a poor person, or a destitute person.

SPIRITUAL SENSES: The deeper meaning of a biblical passage implicitly intended by the human author and explicitly intended by God. The theological tradition subdivides the spiritual senses of Scripture into the allegorical sense, the tropological sense, and the anagogical sense.

TABERNACLE: The tent in which the sacrificial worship of the Lord was carried out from the time of the Sinai Covenant until the building of the Temple under King Solomon.

TEMPLE: The "house for the Lord," proposed by King David and built by King Solomon in Jerusalem. It replaced the Tabernacle as the principal place of worship for the people of Israel.

TENT OF MEETING: The inner sanctuary of the Tabernacle, housing the Bread of Presence, the Altar of Incense, and the Lampstand (Menorah).

TORAH: The first five books of the Bible: Genesis, Exodus, Leviticus, Numbers, and Deuteronomy. In Greek, it is called the *Pentateuch*.

TROPOLOGICAL SENSE: The spiritual sense of Scripture that considers how the literal sense of a passage in the Old Testament can be applied to moral action in our lives here and now. This sense is also sometimes called the Moral Sense.

DAVID THE KING

ANSWER KEY

ANSWER KEY IMAGE

King David. Aert de Gelder, 1683.

Amsterdam. Rijksmuseum Amsterdam.

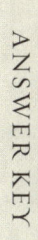

DAVID THE KING

ANSWER KEY

Lesson One: The Law of the Gift   3

Lesson Two: Your Servant is Listening   5

Lesson Three: Warrior of God   7

Lesson Four: Gathered in Jerusalem   9

Lesson Five: The House of David   11

Lesson Six: Absalom, My Son!   13

LESSON ONE – THE LAW OF THE GIFT

✠

1. **What human and spiritual insights can we gain by understanding the authorship of 1-2 Samuel? (CCC 109-114)**

   Context of the time: The human authors of sacred Scripture share much with the authors of any other great work of literature: they lived in a specific place, at a specific time, and flourished in a specific culture. Understanding the historical and cultural milieu of the human authors of Scripture gives us more insight into their writings and into the literal sense of the passage. Also, you cannot fully comprehend the spiritual senses of Scripture unless you first understand the foundation of the literal sense.

   History of Israel: The Deuteronomist pulled together many generations of the history of Israel to share in more detail the story of our salvation. It is important to understand the lineage of Jesus and how the faith journey of the Israelites led to the coming of the Messiah.

2. **Summarize the literal and spiritual meanings of the story of Hannah (1 Sam 1:1-28; CCC 115-119)**

   Literal sense: Hannah is one of the wives of Elkanah, and is unable to bear children. Because of her barrenness, Hannah is mercilessly teased by his other wife, Peninnah. One year, while in Shiloh to offer the yearly sacrifice, Hannah was worshipping at the tabernacle when the high priest, Eli, mistakes her for an alcoholic. She explains that she is entirely sober and that she has been praying for deliverance from her barrenness. Eli intercedes for her and she conceives and bears a son, Samuel. Thereafter she sings a song praising and exulting the Lord for raising her up from the lowliness of a childless woman. Hannah then consecrates Samuel to the Lord as a Nazirite to grow up and serve in the temple at Shiloh.

   Spiritual senses: In the allegorical sense, Hannah's physical barrenness represents the spiritual barrenness of Israel as it awaits the Savior. Hannah's prayer, mistaken for drunkenness, represents her being full of the Holy Spirit. Hannah's offering of Samuel to the Lord as a Nazirite prefigures Mary's offering of Jesus as a sacrifice to God the Father.

   In the tropological or moral sense, Hannah exhibits the law of the gift. The more Hannah gives herself away, the more she gives herself to the Lord in prayer, and the more she offers up her much-desired son to the Lord through the Nazirite vow, the more she receives (esteem, honor, a place in salvation history).

   In the anagogical sense, every time we give ourselves away as a sacrifice to the Lord, we enter into a greater share of the divine life.

3. **How does the story of Hannah serve as an allegory of Mary?**

   Both Mary and Hannah were very humble and faithful women, putting God and his purposes first

DAVID THE KING

in their own lives. Hannah, whose name means, "[God] has shown favor," prefigures Mary, who is "blessed among women." Both were full of the Holy Spirit.

Hannah's offering of Samuel to the Lord as a Nazirite represents Mary's offering of Jesus as a sacrifice to God the Father. Just as Hannah offered Samuel in such a way that Samuel's life became a sacrifice, so when Mary learned that "you yourself a sword shall pierce" (Luke 2:35), she offered herself as a sacrifice united to her Son, whose whole life would be offered to God on the cross.

As Bishop Barron notes, the deepest union between Hannah and Mary is evident in the songs that each holy woman sings. These songs describe the pattern according to which God's gracious action unfolds in history. They begin with praise: "My heart exults in the Lord," says Hannah; "My soul magnifies the Lord," says Mary. They continue with an acknowledgement of our own humility before God and our need for him. "My strength is exalted in the Lord," says Hannah; "He has looked with favor on his lowly servant," says Mary. They then describe that what has happened to them is a microcosm of the entire pattern by which God relates to humanity: putting down the mighty, exalting the lowly, filling the hungry, making the poor rich. Each woman sees in herself a figure of God's love for his entire people, even as she prepares to raise a son who will bear concrete witness to God's mercy. On account of Hannah's sacrifice, Samuel will grow up as a prophet, priest, and ruler of Israel—moreover, he will anoint the paradigmatic king of Israel, David. On account of Mary's sacrifice, Jesus will grow up as the fulfillment of all prophecy, priesthood, and kingship as the *Messiah*, the anointed one of God.

4. **What is the "law of the gift"? Give some examples from Scripture and your own life to illustrate this law.**

   Bishop Barron shows us how this Marian paradigm gives us a law according to which God governs the entire metaphysical and moral order: the law of the gift. "The law of the gift," Bishop Barron explains, "is a metaphysical and spiritual principle, and it runs like this: your being increases in the measure that you give it away."

   Some examples from Scripture (there are many others) are:

   Hannah: Gave her firstborn son, Samuel, back to God by consecrating him to the Temple. Now she is remembered as a key figure in restoring Israel to right worship by mothering a great prophet.

   Ruth: Gave away the comfort of her homeland to return with her mother-in-law to Israel. Became the wife of Boaz, and their son became the grandfather of David, the king.

   Mary: Gave her life totally to bring Jesus into the world, and is now called "blessed" by all the nations. Was assumed into heaven and became the Queen of Heaven, the privileged mother of the eternal King.

   Joseph: Gave up his pride and his idea of married life to take Mary into his home and protect her and Jesus. Now is revered as one of the greatest and most humble saints.

   The Apostles: Gave up home and family to follow Jesus and now reign in heaven alongside him.

LESSON TWO – YOUR SERVANT IS LISTENING

✠

1. **What were the three ways in which Phinehas and Hophni sinned against the Lord? (1 Sam 2:12-17, 22)**

   a. They took more than their prescribed share of the meat from the sacrificial offerings.
   b. They often asked for the meat raw, before it was boiled, so they could roast it and enjoy the flavor of the fat. Mosaic law prescribed that all offerings should be boiled and eaten without fat.
   c. They had sexual relations with women who came to the Temple and who were not their wives.

2. **In what ways did Eli fail to fulfill his role as priest and judge? (1 Sam 2:23-25, 27-29; 3:11-14; Lev 5:20-26; Lev 18:20; 20:10; Lev 16)**

   As a father and a judge, he did not go far enough to stop the sinfulness of his sons. As the high priest, he refused to intercede for them through a guilt offering for their theft and through the annual ritual for grave sins (i.e., the adultery) on the Day of Atonement. He did not repent and change his actions when he heard the word of God given to him twice: first by a "man of God" and then by young Samuel, the new prophet of Israel.

3. **Summarize the differences in the Old Testament priesthood of Eli's time and the New Testament priesthood of today. (CCC 1539-1540, 1544-1545; Heb 9:11-14; CCC 613)**

   - In Eli's time, only men from the tribe of Levi were allowed to be priests and serve liturgically, according to the Mosaic law. The current priesthood includes men from every nation and ethnicity.

   - Old Testament priests offered various types of sacrifices (i.e., cereal offerings, peace offerings, sin offerings and guilt offerings) repeatedly for the atonement of sins, but these offerings were "powerless to bring about salvation" (CCC 1540). Old Testament offerings were either animals or fruits of the field. Current priests stand "in the person of Christ" at the Mass and re-present the once and for all sacrifice that Christ accomplished with his own body on the cross for the forgiveness of our sins—past, present, and future. It is the only sacrifice that brings salvation.

     > The redemptive sacrifice of Christ is unique, accomplished once for all; yet it is made present in the Eucharistic sacrifice of the Church. The same is true of the one priesthood of Christ; it is made present through the ministerial priesthood without diminishing the uniqueness of Christ's priesthood: "Only Christ is the true priest, the others being only his ministers" (CCC 1545).

4. **How was God working for the benefit of Israel through the troubled time of Eli and his sons? (1 Sam 2:26; 3:1-10, 19-21)**

   God was raising up a great prophet, Samuel, right under Eli's nose in the Temple. God spoke to Samuel personally and instructed him to take his words to Eli and to all of Israel. Soon Israel accepted him as a true prophet of God because "the Lord was with him, not permitting any word of his to go unfulfilled" (1 Sam 3:19).

LESSON THREE – WARRIOR OF GOD

✠

1. **What was wrong with the Israelites' request for a king? (1 Sam 8:4-9, 19-20; Deut 33:1-5)**

   They rejected the fact that God was their one and only king, and also rejected the judicial system that God had provided. The Israelites explained why they were requesting a king: "that we also may be like all the nations, and that our king may govern us and go out before us and fight our battles" (1 Sam 8:20). If we consider these words against the background of the judicial system, we can see that they constitute a drastic lack of fidelity to the Deuteronomic Covenant. It was the Lord who governed the people and gave them the judicial system, it was the Lord who raised up the judges, it was the Lord who empowered the judges, and it was the Lord who ensured the victory of the judges against their enemies. So in a sense, refusing the Lord in this way was an act of idolatry.

2. **What were the two sins that got the kingship taken away from Saul? (1 Sam 10:2-8; 13:8-13; 15:1-9)**

   1. Saul is to wait seven days until Samuel arrives to sacrifice a burnt offering in Gilgal, but he sacrifices it before Samuel arrives.
   2. Saul does not put the ban totally on the Amalekites. The ban involved the complete destruction of whatever was under it. This means that the Israelites were commanded to destroy all the people and all the spoils of war, to take nothing for themselves. However, Saul kept some people as slaves and some livestock for himself and the Israelites.

3. **How does David's battle with Goliath illustrate the principle *gratia prima* ("grace first"), and how do soldiers of God fight? (1 Sam 16:13; 1 Sam 17:37-51; CCC 2008-2010; CCC 2306)**

   In his heart, David trusted in the Lord and loved him faithfully. Before the battle, he had been anointed as the future king, and the "spirit rushed upon him." So he had received and accepted God's grace before he ventured into battle with Goliath. God chooses us first and gives us the grace to accomplish his purposes for us. All we have to do is cooperate.

   Soldiers of God fight nonviolently, as Christ did on the cross. David is a good example of this approach, as he came at Goliath naked and with only a slingshot and five stones. Goliath advanced first, and David acted in defense of the Israelites and in cooperation with God's grace.

4. **How is David a figure of Christ? (Acts 13:22; Ps 119:2-3, 47-48)**

   When God replaced Saul with David, he called David "a man after my own heart" and said that David would "carry out my every wish" (Acts 13:22). Jesus was one with God and became man. He fulfilled the will of God the Father and carried out his every wish, even suffering and dying on the cross.

   David was humble, as was Christ. David was faithful to the Lord, and when he was not, he repented and accepted the consequences.

David is an anointed man of God and Christ is the Messiah, which means "anointed one." David was both a priest and a king; Jesus was a priest, prophet, and king.

Another thing that points us to see Christ in David is the manner in which he does battle against Goliath. Owing to his complete fidelity to the Lord, David is unafraid to do battle naked. David's nakedness represents the nakedness of Christ who conquers sin and the hosts of Satan, armed only with the power of God.

LESSON FOUR – GATHERED IN JERUSALEM

✠

1. **Why is Saul envious of David? How does Saul's envy contribute to David's rise? (1 Sam 18:6-9, 25-30; 19:1-2, 11-12, 18-24)**

   The beginning of Saul's envy springs from David's conquests in battle: "Saul has slain his thousands, David his tens of thousands" (1 Sam 18:7), and "his name was held in great esteem" (1 Sam 18:30).

   Saul attempts to thwart David and even have him killed; however, many of his attempts actually help David survive and grow in popularity. Saul instructs David to do battle with the Philistines and bring back evidence of the death of 200 of these enemies. Saul promises that David can marry his daughter, Michal, if he accomplishes this task, secretly hoping that David is killed in the battle. David succeeds and marries Michal, who loves David and becomes very loyal to him, even warning him when she knows of her father's plans to kill him. In addition, David develops a very close friendship with Saul's son, Jonathan, who protects him and helps him escape Saul's death traps.

   David goes to visit the prophet Samuel, and Saul sends men to arrest him there. However, the men fall under a "prophetic ecstasy" and would not arrest him. Finally, Saul comes himself and also falls into this "prophetic ecstasy."

2. **Why won't David kill Saul, and why does David kill the man who claims to have done so? (1 Sam 24:5-8; 26:8-11; 31:1-4; 2 Sam 1:6-10, 13-16)**

   David will not kill Saul because Saul is an "anointed one" of God, and he believes that no one can "lay a hand on the Lord's anointed and remain innocent" (1 Sam 26:9). For the same reason, David kills the Amalekite, who claimed to have killed Saul to receive glory from David. David said to the Amalekite, "Your blood is on your head, for you testified against yourself when you said, 'I put the Lord's anointed to death'" (2 Sam 1:16).

3. **How and why did David establish his capital in Jerusalem? (Judg 2:20-23; 2 Sam 5:6-12)**

   David had to invade and conquer Jerusalem first before he could establish it as the capital of his kingdom. From a human perspective, David may have chosen Jerusalem to pay homage to Saul, as it was his city (tribe of Benjamin). Also, it was very centrally located, which served David's purposes of reuniting all twelve tribes in the capital city.

   In a spiritual sense, the city fell to David although other Israelites had failed to conquer it because he was faithful to God and to God's covenant with Israel. God had not allowed the Israelites to take and retain full possession of the promised land due to their transgressions during the time of the flight from Egypt, and at the present time it was inhabited by the Jebusites. The city was virtually impenetrable; however, with God's help, David captured it by attacking through the "water shaft."

4. **Why does David not put on the ephod until after he conquers Jerusalem? How does the fact that David is king but also becomes a priest affect the Levitical priesthood? (Gen 14:18; 2 Sam 6:14, 17-18; Ps 110:1-4; 2 Sam 8:18; Heb 7:11-14; CCC 1539)**

   David was not a priest, so he could not by Law wear the ephod, a holy garment of priests. After the procession with the Ark arrives in Jerusalem, David takes the ephod and puts it on. "David was belted with a linen ephod….[and] David offered burnt offerings and peace offerings before the Lord. And when David had finished offering the burnt offerings and the peace offerings, he blessed the people in the name of the Lord of hosts" (2 Sam 6:14, 17-18).

   Along with Jerusalem, David inherited the ancient office of the priest-king Melchizedek, as Jerusalem was the ancient seat of his priesthood. As Hebrews 7:11-14 explains, reestablishing the order of Melchizedek was necessary to overcome the shortcomings of the Levitical priesthood. In this way, David represents an initial fulfillment of God's promise to replace Eli with a faithful priest.

5. **Who ultimately fulfills the prophecy, "You are a priest forever according to the order of Melchizedek"? (Ps 110:4). What can we expect to gain from this great high priest? (Heb 7:22-27; CCC 1544)**

   Jesus Christ is the ultimate fulfillment of the prophecy from Psalm 110. Jesus was himself the sacrifice and the great high priest, and so is the eternal guarantee of the new covenant between humankind and God. "He is always able to save those who approach God through him, since he lives forever to make intercession for them" (Heb 7:25).

LESSON FIVE – THE HOUSE OF DAVID

✠

1. **What is the Davidic Covenant revealed in Nathan's prophecy? (2 Sam 7:1-16) Why does God grant David "a rest from his enemies"? (Deut 12:1-12)**

    The Davidic Covenant is God's promise to King David to grant him a royal dynasty of descendants that will be firm forever. God says through the prophet Nathan:

    > I will make your name like that of the greatest on earth. Moreover, the LORD also declares to you that the LORD will make a house for you: when your days have been completed and you rest with your ancestors, I will raise up your offspring after you, sprung from your loins, and I will establish his kingdom. He it is who shall build a house for my name, and I will establish his royal throne forever. I will be a father to him, and he shall be a son to me. If he does wrong, I will reprove him with a human rod and with human punishments; but I will not withdraw my favor from him as I withdrew it from Saul who was before you. Your house and your kingdom are firm forever before me; your throne shall be firmly established forever (2 Sam 7:9-16).

    God gave David "rest from all his enemies round about" (2 Sam 7:1). These words are full of significance in the Deuteronomistic History. They represent the fulfillment of God's charge to the Israelites to cast out idolatry from the land and of God's promise to reward the Israelites for doing so. David accomplished just that.

2. **Why doesn't David get to build the Temple in Jerusalem? (2 Sam 7:12-15; 1 Chron 22:8)**

    God tells the prophet Nathan to tell David *not* to build a Temple in Jerusalem, as he had planned. As Bishop Barron points out, the Lord forbids David to build a temple for the Lord because David had spent too much time at war: "You have shed much blood and have waged great wars; you shall not build a house to my name, because you have shed so much blood before me upon the earth" (1 Chron 22:8).

3. **Why would people in the time of the Babylonian Captivity write about God's promises to David? (1 Chron 22:9-10; 2 Sam 12:24; 1 Kings 1:39; 1 Kings 6:1)**

    David interpreted the covenant Nathan had communicated to be speaking about Solomon (1 Chron 22:9), although Nathan never mentioned Solomon by name when he communicated God's words to David. During the Babylonian Captivity, the Israelites looked to God's promise to David as a sure foundation from which they could hope for the renewal of Israel. Even if the restoration of the Davidic dynasty seemed well nigh impossible, if the people could find even a sliver of trust in God, they could—and did—latch onto God's promise to David, confirmed by the events of Solomon's life, as a sure sign that God had not and would not forsake them forever.

DAVID THE KING

Seeing the promised son as Solomon gave the people of Israel a reason to hope. By the time of the Babylonian Captivity, they could see in hindsight that Solomon had apparently satisfied all of the criteria of Nathan's prophecy in 2 Samuel 7:

"I will raise up your offspring after you, who shall come forth from your body"
  (fulfilled in 2 Sam 12:24)
"I will establish his kingdom" (fulfilled in 1 Kings 1:39)
"He shall build a house for my name" (fulfilled in 1 Kings 6)

For this reason, the people could look to the history of Solomon's rule as a fulfillment of the prophecy confirming God's promise of an everlasting line to David.

4. **Why do we believe, as did St. Augustine, that the promise of a perpetual heir in the Davidic Covenant refers to Jesus? (Matt 1:1-17; Luke 1:32-33, 67-72; 2:1-5)**

From the genealogies in the Gospels of both Matthew and Luke, it is clearly revealed that Jesus is descended from the House of David. In Matthew, there are three sets of 14 generations from Abraham to Jesus. In Hebrew the same characters are used for letters and numbers, and the name "David" is synonymous with the number 14.

Luke's Gospel also affirms Jesus' Davidic identity through the witness of two important figures who give testimony to Jesus' Davidic ancestry: the archangel Gabriel (Luke 1:32-33), and John the Baptist's father, Zechariah (Luke 1:67-72). Luke also references historical records of the census, and that Joseph traveled to the city of David (Bethlehem) because "he was of the house and family of David" (Luke 2:4).

Finally, no human dynasty could continue in perpetuity; only the everlasting kingdom of God could truly fulfill Nathan's prophecy.

LESSON SIX – ABSALOM, MY SON!

✠

1. **What are the two greatest commandments, and how does David honor them before the incident with Bathsheba? (Deut 6:4-5; Matt 22:36-40; 1 Kings 15:5; 2 Sam 9:1-10)**

   The Israelites often repeated and emphasized the greatest commandment, called the *Shema*:

   > Hear, O Israel! The LORD is our God, the LORD alone! Therefore, you shall love the LORD, your God, with your whole heart, and with your whole being, and with your whole strength (Deut 6:4-5).

   When asked what is the greatest commandment, Jesus quoted the *Shema* and emphasized that loving our neighbor as ourselves was closely related to the first and greatest commandment:

   > You shall love the Lord, your God, with all your heart, with all your soul, and with all your mind. The second is like it: You shall love your neighbor as yourself (Matt 22:37, 39).

   Before the incident with Bathsheba, in which David committed two mortal sins (adultery and murder), he lived peerlessly according to both of these commandments:

   - He defended God's people in countless battles, starting with his fight with Goliath. In all these battles, he followed God's will and sought to eliminate nations that practiced idolatry so Israel could keep their covenant with the Lord. David set about "doing battle with evil all the way down," as Bishop Barron states.
   - He spared Saul's life twice while at war with him and while knowing Saul's intention to kill him because Saul had been anointed king by God.
   - For the sake of Saul's son, Jonathan, David seeks out a member of the house of Saul to whom he can show kindness. He finds Mephibosheth, a son of Jonathan, who is lame in both feet. Out of purely gratuitous love David lavishes him with the entire wealth of Saul's house, and grants him the privilege of always eating at David's table.
   - He prayed often, repented, and followed God's instructions as given to him directly or through the prophet Nathan.
   - His faithfulness was confirmed in the fact that he was able to overtake and occupy Jerusalem when so many others before him had failed. When David brought the Ark into Jerusalem, he showed the depth of his love in his heart and soul by leading a liturgical procession that included his own dancing and singing.
   - As a godly king, he established the "center of right praise" in Jerusalem and united all the tribes of Israel to worship the one true God. He led Israel to worship God, not to worship false gods or himself as king.

2. **How does David's sin with Bathsheba mirror Adam's sin in the Garden of Eden? (2 Sam 11:1-17; Gen 3:1-7; CCC 397-398)**

   Both Adam and David disobeyed God and chose to put their own desires for pleasure ahead of God's commandments. Adam was enticed by the forbidden fruit and went against the Lord's

DAVID THE KING

command not to eat from the Tree of the Knowledge of Good and Evil. David was enticed by the beauty of Bathsheba and committed adultery with her. Then he committed murder by sending her husband into battle to be abandoned on the front lines and killed by the enemy.

Speaking of Original Sin, the *Catechism* says:

> Man tempted by the devil, let his trust in his Creator die in his heart and, abusing his freedom, disobeyed God's command… In that sin man *preferred* himself to God and by that very act scorned him. He chose himself over and against God (CCC 397-398).

3. **What are the four consequences that Nathan promises to David? How are they fulfilled in David's subsequent interactions with his children? (2 Sam 12:9-12; 13; 14:33; 15:10-12, 13-16; 16:20-22)**

The four consequences of David's mortal sins that Nathan promises are (2 Sam 12:9-12):

1. "The sword shall never depart from your house…"
2. "I will raise up evil against you out of your own house…"
3. "I will take your wives before your eyes…"
4. "And [I will] give them to your neighbor…and [your neighbor] shall lie with your wives in the sight of this sun."

The consequences are fulfilled as follows:

1. David's son, Amnon, rapes his half-sister, Tamar, and David does not reprimand him strongly enough and punish him according to the law. Absalom, David's son and blood brother of Tamar, seeks revenge and has Amnon killed. David forgives Absalom after a few years without true repentance from his son (2 Sam 13; 2 Sam 14:33).
2. Absalom plots to become king and rebels against David, so David's throne is threatened from within, not from a foreign power (2 Sam 15:10-12).
3. Upon hearing of Absalom's betrayal and mounting popularity, David decides to flee Jerusalem, leaving ten of his concubines behind to care for the palace. Thus he is separated from his "wives" (2 Sam 15:13-16).
4. When Absalom arrives in Jerusalem, he has sexual relations with David's ten concubines, thus humiliating David and further asserting his own authority (2 Sam 16:20-22).

4. **What spiritual quality allows David to retake Jerusalem and the kingdom? (2 Sam 16:5-12; 18:31-32; 19:1; CCC 1450)**

David's humble and heartfelt repentance allows him to retake Jerusalem and the kingdom.

David sees Shime-i's insults as a divinely appointed penance; David accepts the penance, and offers it up for deliverance from his sin. One senses that David's acceptance of Shime-i represents his acceptance of all the divinely appointed consequences of his actions. This acceptance, together with the contrition that accompanies it, begins to redeem David's situation. It marks the beginning of his return as king, and the beginning of victory.

When news is brought to David of Absalom's death, David evinces no shock. As Bishop Barron describes, he is fully aware that this situation is his own fault, that the death of his son is one possible consequence, and he has already accepted with contrition the consequences of his sins, offering them up to the Lord in expiation for his sins. When he receives the terrible news of his son's death, he responds not with shock but with sorrow.

Through David's contrition, his resignation to the will of God, his penitential spirit, and the expiatory power of his sufferings, David returns to faithfulness in the Lord and so is restored to many of the blessings he previously enjoyed.